A Letter to America

A Letter to America

By David Boren

WITH A NEW POSTSCRIPT BY THE AUTHOR

UNIVERSITY OF OKLAHOMA PRESS : NORMAN

Library of Congress Cataloging-in-Publication Data

Boren, David, 1941–

A letter to America / By David Boren.

p. cm.

Includes bibliographical references.

ISBN 978-0-8061-3944-9 (hardcover : alk. paper)

ISBN 978-0-8061-4202-9 (pbk : alk. paper)

1. Political planning—United States.

2. United States—Politics and government—2001–

I. Title.

JK468.P64B72 2008

320.60973—dc22

2007046722

To the students
at the University of Oklahoma
and their generation
of Americans

Contents

Acknowledgments

This book would not have been possible without the constant love and support of my wife and best friend, Molly Shi Boren. She strongly encouraged the writing of the book and helped in its editing. I also want to thank my daughter, Carrie, and my son, Dan, for their support.

Many friends and colleagues have also provided invaluable help and advice. I express my profound appreciation to them. They include David McCullough, Sherry Evans, Blake Rambo, Tripp Hall, Nick Hathaway, Joe Harroz, Josh Galper, Craig Lavoie, Catherine Bishop, Donald Lamm, Bob Burke, Nick Kotz, Dorothy Massey, Zach Messitte, Ann and Jeff Bingaman, Shad Satterthwaite, Jim Lehrer, Sam Nunn, Richard Sandor, Ruth Simmons, Steve Gillon, Eric Liu, David Levy, Keith Gaddie, Howard Lamar, Barbara DeSantis, Walter H. Helmerich III, David Burrage, Jon Stuart, Henry Zarrow, Cy Wagner, Michael Price, Gene Rainbolt, Curtis Mewbourne, Michael Burrage, Charles Stephenson, DeVier Pierson, Stratton Taylor, Ty Trippett, Joel Jankowsky, Steve Burrage, Max Berry, Richard Bell, Tom Clark, Rick Dunning, Sean Burrage, John Massey, Reggie Whitten, and from the University of Oklahoma Press, Byron Price,

Charles Rankin, and Dale Bennie. The help and inspiration of all those named and many others, including my students, were indispensable to this effort.

David Boren
Norman, Oklahoma
February 15, 2008

A Letter to America

Dear American,

This letter is to you. If I were mailing it to you in an envelope, it would be marked URGENT. The country we love is in trouble. In truth we are in grave danger of declining as a nation. If we do not act quickly, that decline will become dramatic.

The signs of trouble are clear for all to see. Only those in deliberate denial could fail to notice.

For over thirty years as a state legislator, governor, U.S. senator, and university president, I have been given a chance to closely observe and sometimes be involved in decisions that have influenced what has happened in our country. For six years as chair of the Senate Select Committee on Intelligence, I had the opportunity to study very sensitive intelligence assessments of the challenges we face. As a university president, I have had the chance to step back and observe our nation's direction from a more objective and reflective vantage point. I've also been able to listen to the hopes and aspirations of the current generation of young Americans.

Those who have been given opportunities to observe have an obligation to share with others what they have learned. Sharing with you what I have seen and learned is the modest objective of this letter. As Americans, we don't talk with each other often enough about things that really matter.

Three or four years ago I was serving on the Rhodes Scholarship Selection Committee for our area. The committee was interviewing an incredibly talented group of finalists for the scholarship. Almost by chance, I asked the first candidate, "How long do you think the United States will be the world's leading superpower?" The candidate had already answered with great quickness and eloquence a host of difficult questions ranging from the arts to science and philosophy. He had demonstrated depth of thought and strong powers of analysis. Now, in response to my question he was struck silent. On his face was a look of shock. Although he continued to remain awkwardly silent, I could sense his desire to blurt out, "Forever," or at least, "For all of my life." He seemed bewildered that I would suggest that American dominance might not continue forever. Finally, in an effort to be helpful, I said, "Surely you realize that American dominance will not last forever." I pointed out that the Roman, Ottoman, and British empires had not lasted forever. I also pointed out that the United States has only 6 percent of the world's population and that China and India combined have ten times our population. Still he was silent. Again, in an effort to help him, I said, "Perhaps we could focus on some of the areas you feel will determine how long we will be a major influence in the world."

Slowly he began to talk about the need for excellence in education, the need to stop piling up large budget deficits, and the need to reduce cynicism about politics.

Compared to his other responses, his answers to my question came haltingly. Clearly he had never contemplated the possibility that America might not always lead the world.

As the day of interviews continued, I posed the same question to each succeeding candidate. In each case, the result was virtually the same. At the end of the day, I found myself haunted by the failure of the very best and brightest among us to focus on the things that would determine our future. I wondered why the candidates had not thought about these issues many times before the interviews. It was obvious that our educational system was not encouraging them to think about these issues. Our social conversations had not included them. Our media had certainly not confronted them with the policy choices we must make.

That experience finally caused me to write this letter to you. It has been late in coming. Procrastination is but one of my failings. In my defense, I was also distracted by a host of other civic and family responsibilities and by innumerable problems that confront the president of any large public university. Perhaps it was the irrelevance of most of the public discussion in a crucial presidential election year that finally caused me to put pen to paper.

The history of our country demonstrates that we Americans are natural problem solvers. Again and again, when we have come to understand the problems we face, we have come together to find a way to solve them. Our greatest leaders have not met the challenges and solved these problems by themselves. These leaders were teachers who educated us as Americans about the problems we needed to solve. The challenges were met and the problems were overcome by the American people themselves.

Great leaders have helped lead us through times that threatened our very existence as a nation. George Washington's small band of troops held together in the winter of 1776–77 when our national independence was almost snuffed out only months after it was proclaimed. The Great Depression of the 1930s produced social chaos that in other nations led to political dictatorship. In contrast, the United States survived the crisis with creative programs such as the Works Progress Administration (WPA), which gave Americans the chance to work instead of making them dependent on welfare. After the devastating attack on Pearl Harbor, all of the American people mobilized to win a dangerous war on two fronts. Waves of volunteers young and old poured into military recruiting stations; and civilians—many of them women symbolized by Rosie the Riveter—went to work in defense plants. A strong sense of justice coupled with a commitment to nonviolence and the integrity of our independent court system brought us through a civil rights revolution in the 1960s that in other societies might have led to civil war along racial lines.

Once problems and challenges become clear, Americans find ways to unite to solve them. Challenges have always brought out the best in us. At this moment we desperately need leaders who have the courage to tell us what we need to know. We Americans are ready to hear the truth, and we have the spirit to do what needs to be done.

Since the terrorist attacks of September 11, 2001, the attitude of people around the world toward the United States has radically changed. In the days immediately following the attacks, an outpouring of support for America came from every corner of the globe. But this has since changed. Sadly, the French newspaper *Le Monde*'s famous headline the day after the tragedies in New York, Pennsylvania, and Washington—"We Are All Americans"—is now a distant memory. Respect for our country has dropped at an alarming rate. In some countries, support for the United States has dropped by 50 percent or more. The 94 percent of the world's population that lives outside the United States will not automatically follow our lead.

We've seen example after example of the destabilization of societies when the middle class disappears and nations are left divided between their rich and poor. Year after year we watch as our middle class shrinks; disparities in income are now at their highest levels in the United States since 1929. What is our strategy for reversing this trend?

Forty other countries now have a higher life expectancy than the United States, in no small part because 45 million Americans have no health insurance. When will we act?

For the first time in our history, most Americans—almost two-thirds—no longer believe that our future will be as good or better than our past! When will we honestly examine the reasons for our national pessimism? When will we ask ourselves what damage this pessimism is doing to our national will, our tenacity, and our vision? Today too many politicians play on our fears to attract our votes. We must not forget that we worked our way out of this country's greatest economic crisis by heeding a leader who told us, "The only thing we have to fear is fear itself."

Our political system is broken. Bipartisanship, with the parties working together to solve urgent problems, is viewed with nostalgic romanticism. We seem resigned fatalistically to the idea that such a spirit cannot be revived. Why not? Surely there are leaders who could bring us together again who would not put party before country. It's time to replace pandering partisans with real statesmen, even if it means electing independents to Congress and a nonpartisan, independent president of the United States. The vicious cycle of our increasing political partisanship must be broken.

Grassroots democracy is being destroyed by a flood of special-interest money pouring into politics. The cost of campaigns has risen tenfold in fewer than thirty years. Cynicism is so high that only about 20 percent of Americans believe that Congress represents people like themselves. In congressional districts, representation of special interests has replaced representation of citizens. When will we make campaign finance reform such a strong Main Street issue that Congress will be afraid to stall real reforms? When will we get angry enough to take our government off the auction block where it is for sale to the highest bidder?

Shockingly, we as citizens are becoming incapable of protecting our rights and democratic institutions, because we do not even know our own history. Americans are not educated about the ideas and events that led to the writing of our Constitution or about what generations have done to preserve it. A recent study indicated that half of American high school seniors thought that the United States was aligned with Germany in World War II, and only 64 percent of students at top American universities could name George Washington as the commander of our forces at the Battle of Yorktown. Even at elite universities and colleges, the next generation of the best and brightest fails basic civic literacy. Those who do not even understand their rights will hardly be able to defend them. When will we insist that no student graduate from an American high school or college without enough knowledge of American history and government to function as a citizen?

These are but a few of the challenges we face. The good news is that Americans have an amazingly positive track record when it comes to meeting challenges. We have proven to be resilient, creative, and tenacious in times of crisis. Solutions are available to us. Do we have the political will to spring to action?

Before we can make progress, we must face fundamental issues. For far too long we have allowed ourselves to waste time on frivolous discussions about celebrity, sports, entertainment, and titillating gossip. None of those things will determine our future or that of our children and grandchildren. Every week, I check the local and nationally circulated newspapers for the most-read stories of the past week. Often, I go for weeks without seeing listed among the top ten a single analytical story about an issue of major long-term importance. Surfing television channels reveals hours and hours of breathless cable news stories about the celebrity scandal of the week and other exploits that will soon be forgotten and certainly will not end up in the history books.

We do not have time to waste. Many of the alarming developments facing us are interrelated. If we intend to reassert our leadership in this world in new ways, we must first do something about excessive and petty partisanship. We must come together as we did during and after World War II. If we intend to strengthen the middle class, Congress must become less dependent on campaign money from special-interest groups so that it can distribute more fairly the financial burden of education and health care. Democrats, Republicans, independents—it does not matter; we must develop a coordinated strategy.

For twenty years I immersed myself in the world of politics. For the past twenty-six semesters, I have taught university freshmen an introductory course in American government and politics. My students have rekindled my hope and my idealism. They have become my friends and my colleagues. They have inspired me by their determination to make things better for others and to build strong lasting marriages and families. It is really because of them that I write this letter to you. They deserve to have lives as full and meaningful as those of their parents and grandparents. We must not let them down.

All of us can look back and identify defining choices we made that set our life course for years to come. We are living through a period that will shape life in America and the nation's role in the world for the next century. More than twenty-five years ago, a Zulu chief meeting with me in South Africa said in reference to his own country, "Those who mill about at the crossroads of history do so at their own peril." His warning is relevant to America today.

One of our greatest shortcomings as Americans is our failure to be intellectually curious about what is happening to us as a people. When confronted with alarming news, it seems we seldom ask, Why did this happen? We haven't really stopped to ponder the question of why the attitude of the rest of the world has radically changed. Often I hear people say about those in other nations: "Oh, they just hate us," or "They really dislike us." But how often do we stop to ask why? The implication is that the rest of the world is out of step—not us. Those in other countries may be wrong to dislike us, but do we ever stop to ask why or how they formed such an inaccurate view of us and our motives?

Others' views and feelings about us are clearly important. As I questioned the Rhodes Scholarship candidates, I reminded them that if recent economic trends continue, India and China, for example, will soon build economies that equal our own. Should those countries decide to apply their economic strength to building up their military might, that military power will equal ours, as well. Thus, how other nations feel about us influences our physical security. In addition, more and more jobs in this country depend on our ability to sell our goods and services in the world marketplace.

Because how the rest of the world feels about us is important, we need to think deeply about why its perception has changed so radically. Just six years ago, the majority of people in nearly every other nation approved of the United States and supported our policies. A huge wave of sympathy toward the United States arose after 9/11. A residue of goodwill remained in the noncommunist world for the role we had played in protecting those countries during the Cold War. Our generosity toward others through the Marshall Plan had left among our former enemies a legacy of appreciation and admiration. I'll never forget a conversation I had a few years ago with then–German chancellor Helmut Kohl. He described a day in elementary school soon after the war when, as a hungry child, he received his first good meal, delivered by the U.S. Army. He grew up seeing Americans helping to rebuild his country through the Marshall Plan. With this legacy, how could approval of our country drop in Germany from 78 percent in 2000 to 30 percent today? In Turkey, our longtime NATO ally, approval of the United States fell to 9 percent in 2007.[1] Why are we as a people and why are our leaders not spending time and energy determining why this has happened and what we should do about it?

While we are confronted by startling poll results demonstrating the decline of our standing in the world, we face attitudes here at home that may be even more alarming. Historians and social scientists have often said that the health and strength of a nation or society can be judged by the way its people feel about their future. By that measure, America is in trouble. According to recent polling data, Americans now believe that our best days are behind us.[2] Another recent poll indicated that only 27 percent of Americans believe that we are on the right path. Another poll revealed that more than half of Americans believe their children will grow up to be worse off than they are. In a recent scientific study, 65 percent of Americans said that they are no longer certain their children will have lives as good as their own. Why do we feel as we do? What can we do about it? It is ironic, given the current debate about immigration, that first-generation immigrants are far more likely to be optimistic about America and better lives for their children than are the rest of us. It is also ironic that while we have real incomes twice as high as those of our grandparents, Americans living today are far less satisfied with their lives. Why?

Along with pessimism on a scale never seen before in America has come cynicism. When I resigned from the U.S. Senate two years before the end of my term to become president of the University of Oklahoma, I wanted to learn how my students felt about their own government as compared to how I felt when I was a student at Yale in 1959. Looking back at the data, I found that when I was taking a freshman political science class, about 75 percent of Americans said they usually trusted their government to do what was right. About the same percentage said they believed that Congress cared about people like themselves and reflected their thinking. By the time I started teaching in spring 1995, the percentage of those who had confidence in their political leaders ranged between 10 and 20 percent. In other words, I was teaching a course in American government to a group of students who were deeply cynical about politics and politicians. I grew up viewing public officials with an admiration bordering on awe. I watched my own father, who was a congressman, work to help people who had no place else to turn. From my earliest years, I wanted to be in politics because I believed it was the best way to make a difference in the lives of others. I viewed public officials much as I viewed priests or ministers or rabbis—as men and women who had responded to a calling. Why have attitudes changed so dramatically?

The cynicism surrounding us frightens me far more than outrage would. Our political system is unlikely to be brought down by angry mobs in the streets. Cynicism, on the other hand, undermines the foundations of our political system by leaving people with a sense that they cannot make a difference by getting involved. It is when we stop trying that both our system and our individual liberties are put at great risk. Why are the halls of Congress not ringing, and our own conversations not filled, with debate about the causes of this cynicism?

There are so many important questions that we are not asking ourselves. Three- and four-year-old children constantly ask, Why? why? why? But American adults at the beginning of the twenty-first century seem to have stopped asking the questions that need to be asked.

One reason we do not confront the challenges that will shape our future is that we have forgotten so much about our past. We have developed a case of national amnesia about the ideas, values, and actions that made us great.

In June 2002 Bruce Cole, then chair of the National Endowment for the Humanities, made a speech in which he wisely said: "A nation that does not know why it exists or what it stands for cannot be expected to long endure. . . . We must recover from the amnesia that shrouds our history in darkness, our principles in confusion, and our future in uncertainty. We cannot expect that a nation which has lost its memory will keep its vision. We cannot hope that forgetting our past will enhance our focus on the future."[3] The wisdom of his statement powerfully speaks for itself. More and more, American citizens do not participate in our political system, in part because they do not know how it works and do not know anything about the ideas that shape it. They know nothing of the acts of bravery and courage that sustained our nation in critical times.

Only one-third of college students, according to a recent survey, knew that the Constitution established the division of powers in our political system. If college and university students have so little knowledge of American history and ideas, what about the rest of the population? How secure are our basic rights and liberties enshrined in the Constitution when we as a people know so little about the document itself or how it has been interpreted by the courts in the past two hundred years?

If these questions I have raised seem to imply that you are reading a letter from a harsh critic who has given up on this country, nothing could be further from the truth! Time and time again, through financial crises, world wars, and natural disasters, Americans have proven their inherent strength and determination. We need to prove them again now.

I want American influence to continue in world affairs, because I truly believe it is best not only for us but for the entire human family. Consider the power the United States held at the end of World War II. It had the most powerful military machine in the history of the world, including a monopoly on nuclear weapons. It had more than two-thirds of the economic value of all goods and services moving in world trade. While the twentieth century has been viewed by historians as the "American Century," it was not the century of a new American empire. Instead, the United States used its power to help others around the world achieve their own political and economic freedom. Implementation of the Marshall Plan, which provided financial aid, even to our adversaries in World War II, to rebuild their countries, was one of the wisest and most generous acts in history. Imagine a people taxing themselves to provide aid to those who had been responsible for killing and wounding their sons, daughters, and other family members and for causing economic goods to be rationed at home. Generosity, vision, political courage, and bipartisanship

came together to help America lead the world and ultimately to end the Cold War without a third world war.

How long will the United States remain the world's
leading superpower, or at least one of the world's most
influential nations? The answer depends on our asking
ourselves tough questions, taking an objective look at
ourselves without flinching, and then uniting to meet
the challenges we face. We have no time to spare. We
must act now!

CHAPTER ONE

The United States and the World

Let us return to the question of why approval of the United States in the rest of the world has dropped so dramatically and so quickly. We have spent very little time as a people in examining the reasons. Instead, most of us, including many of our leaders, have simply reacted with anger and hurt feelings. I often find myself doing so. How could they dislike us when we've done so much for them? How could they forget the sacrifices of Americans in such places as Iwo Jima? How could they forget the billions of dollars in food aid, thousands of Peace Corps volunteers, and countless educational opportunities? How could they forget we bore a disproportionate share of the cost to maintain the balance of power and provide security for the entire noncommunist world during the long years of the Cold War?

I believe perceptions of the United States have changed for the worse because we have not led wisely in recent years. We can restore respect for the United States by better understanding what role we should play in world affairs. What should we do to rebuild relationships with the rest of the world? Why must we rebuild those relationships? Because we cannot solve the major challenges confronting us all by ourselves. Health crises and epidemics, environmental problems, criminal activity, and terrorist actions all flow across national boundaries. They are, as former United Nations secretary-general Kofi Annan termed them, "problems without passports." We cannot escape them by walling out the rest of the world. Nor do any of these major threats lend themselves to purely military solutions. Even if they did, this country does not have the military strength to deal with them by ourselves. We must never fail to maintain sufficient military strength to protect our own vital national security interests all by ourselves if we are forced to do so. However, we should be wise enough to avoid ever having to go it alone. We should constantly build partnerships with others so that we will not have to overstretch our national resources or risk the lives only of young Americans.

It is, therefore, extremely important for us to understand why perceptions of the United States have changed. According to a recent Pew Research Center study, people living in Canada, Britain, Germany, and France have more confidence in the global leadership of President Vladimir Putin of Russia than they have in President George W. Bush. Part of the change in attitude toward the United States has been caused by the personal unpopularity of our current president and his policies.

The depth of the change, however, cannot be explained simply by the popularity or unpopularity of individual leaders. The Pew study found that especially among countries that have been our longtime allies, the slide in approval has other causes. More and more nations believe that the United States acts without taking into account their interests as well as our own. To put it bluntly, they feel we don't seek advice or take the needs of our friends into consideration. "Arrogant" is the word used in private to describe us. None of us wants to form a partnership with someone who thinks only of himself, talks but never listens, and respects no one else's suggestions. Recent polling data indicate that 89 percent of French, 83 percent of Canadians, and 74 percent of British believe that the United States does not take into account their interests and views in formulating our foreign policy.[1]

The United States is perceived negatively around the world, in part because we ourselves have not figured out our appropriate role in the world since the end of the Cold War. During the Cold War we had a clear mission. We led the free world with a steady hand and a clear vision, protecting freedom and democracy from communist domination by the Soviet Union. We were prepared to make sacrifices to preserve our basic values and our national security while providing an umbrella of security for our allies. We developed military, political, and economic alliances to contain communism, including the North Atlantic Treaty Organization (NATO) in Europe and the Southeast Asia Treaty Organization (SEATO).

In the brief period following the end of World War II, the United States and our allies together developed a clear blueprint that guided our major decisions. It was understood by leaders and citizens alike not only in the United States but in other nations as well.

That blueprint included the doctrines of deterrence

and containment. It was understood that the United States would maintain a balance of power so that the Soviet Union would not be tempted to invade its neighbors or use nuclear weapons irresponsibly. Henry Kissinger called it the "delicate balance of terror." The blueprint also included the Marshall Plan, undertaken to help European nations recover so that they would not be susceptible to the political siren song of communism. In addition, under the Truman Doctrine, another part of this blueprint, the USSR was to be contained within its borders and not allowed to expand geographically. American military forces were strategically placed so as to act as a trip wire to discourage Soviet aggression. Near the end of the Cold War, the Reagan Doctrine enhanced the containment policy by providing that if the Soviets tried to move anywhere in the world, they would be forced to pay an unacceptably high price for their military initiatives. To exact that price from the Soviets in places like Afghanistan, Angola, and Nicaragua, the United States used surrogates supported by American weapons and training. Some called the Afghan War "Russia's Vietnam."

A combination of these policies, all part of a single coherent blueprint, helped bankrupt the Soviet Union both financially and morally and hastened the end of the Cold War. This blueprint was so coherent and well understood that Dean Acheson, secretary of state in the Truman administration, titled his Pulitzer Prize–winning autobiography *Present at the Creation*. Readers instantly recognized the title as referring to the creation of our comprehensive Cold War strategy. While there were certainly mistakes made during the long period of the Cold War, including our ill-conceived intervention in Vietnam and the shameful period in domestic politics known as McCarthyism, the overall consistency of our course of action was remarkable.

As the Cold War came to an end, then-president George H. W. Bush spoke hopefully of a "New World Order." Under this new order the leading nations of the world would cooperate to organize inspection teams to reduce the spread of weapons of mass destruction and build joint military forces to deal with regional military conflicts so that they would not expand. Additional partnerships for free trade and to improve the environment were also advocated. Tragically, no New World Order was created. Now, almost two decades after the end of the Cold War, the world is more dangerous than ever.

In previous foreign-policy debates, Americans divided themselves between "internationalists" who favored engagement with the rest of the world and "isolationists" who mainly believed that we could avoid the problems around us by simply ignoring them and not involving ourselves in their solution.

Today, the divisions appear more often between those who want us to act largely alone in the world—the unilateralists—and those who believe we should act in cooperation and partnership with others—the multilateralists. The results in Vietnam and more recently in Iraq have certainly not strengthened the case for acting largely alone.

Words Abraham Lincoln spoke in 1862 hauntingly remind us that "we cannot escape history." He warned that we will be judged by our action and by our inaction. None of us knows how long the opportunity will last in which to build new partnerships. How long will we have a world not divided between warring power blocs?

One thing is heartbreakingly clear: no leader today could write an autobiography titled *Present at the Creation*. American leaders have developed no new blueprint, no comprehensive architecture for dealing with the times in which we live. There is no plan that corresponds to the wise conceptual thinking that provided relative safe passage through a period of grave danger with threats of mass destruction.

Instead, our foreign policy has been marked by ad hoc interventions and relationships. During the Cold War, when we were the leader of the free world, our allies needed our protection and treated us with loyalty and respect. With the outside threat of the Soviet Union now gone, they no longer tend to accept our policies automatically. We are like parents shocked when their offspring reach a level of development sufficient to think for themselves. Ideally, a relationship built on parental authority later gives way to a friendship built on love and mutual respect. As a nation we must make adjustments to new situations.

Immediately after the end of the Cold War, it was widely believed that we were the world's only superpower and that what we could accomplish had virtually no limits. But who are we now? If we are no longer the undisputed leader of the free world, what is our role today? In a sense, we are experiencing a national identity crisis.

In some ways we still remain, at least in military terms, the world's largest superpower. However, we already have strong economic rivals, and in time they can become military rivals as well. Our unipolar world is rapidly become multipolar. Without our trading relationships with Mexico and Canada, it is likely that the European Union would have already surpassed us as the world's largest market. Nations tend to try to get along with those other nations that control the largest markets into which they hope to sell their goods and services.

While we beat our chests and proclaim ourselves the world's largest superpower, it is foolish to expect that we Americans, with only 6 percent of the world's population, can automatically impose our will on everyone else.

I vividly remember conversations I had with then-president George H. W. Bush and his national security adviser, General Brent Scowcroft, near the end of the first Persian Gulf War. I was chair of the U.S. Senate's Select Committee on Intelligence. We had just swept the forces of Saddam Hussein out of Kuwait. Little stood between our forces and Baghdad. I urged them to finish the job by taking over Iraq and removing Saddam from power. The senior President Bush forcefully disagreed. He first asked me to describe my exit strategy. I admitted that I did not have a good one. He and General Scowcroft then educated me about the long-standing division between the Kurds, Shiites, and Sunnis. They argued that Iraq would disintegrate into civil war, making it difficult for us to leave. Finally, they spoke of the balance of power in the Middle East and explained that the implosion of Iraq would tend only to strengthen the power of Iran in the region and place in greater jeopardy both Israel and moderate Arab states friendly to the United States.

Those conversations changed my mind about what we should do. Clearly this situation did not have an American solution. I came to realize that not every international situation has a purely American solution. Not every country has the preconditions necessary to make a political system just like ours work in its environment. High levels of education, a history of economic freedom, a certain level of wealth, and deep traditions of political and religious tolerance are needed.

John Stuart Mill, in his invaluable essay "On Liberty," emphasizes that liberty is central to the creative vitality of any society. Building upon Mill's thesis, Fareed Zakaria points out in his provocative book *The Future of Freedom* that democracy does not automatically lead to enhanced freedom. The Palestinian elections in 2006, for example, brought Hamas to power. Freedom for religious and political dissenters has hardly been enhanced. If freedom is to be expanded, democracy must be joined with many other elements, including an independent judiciary and specific rights for racial and religious minorities. It is wrong for us to think that the establishment of democracy by itself will lead to stable and free societies.

All good gardeners know that it takes the right temperature range, soil composition, amount of rainfall, and number of hours of sunshine for a particular plant to flourish. It would be foolish to plant a palm tree in the cold climate of Canada. Similarly, political institutions function differently in various cultural settings. Edmund Burke taught us well that political institutions grow and evolve over time. They are not instant creations.

The depth of understanding of the Middle East demonstrated by the first President Bush and his team, including General Scowcroft, Secretary of State James Baker, and General Colin Powell, is clearly demonstrated by the contrasting outcomes of the two wars involving Iraq. During the first gulf war our leaders worked hard to avoid upsetting the balance of power in the Middle East. They followed policies not likely to inflame historic divisions between Shiites, Sunnis, and Kurds. They created no power vacuum inside Iraq. Instead, they built a broad coalition and acted to reaffirm the rule of law and international cooperation. They assiduously avoided turning the conflict into one between the Muslim and non-Muslim worlds. Care was taken to ensure that the coalition troops that first saw military action in the first gulf war were from Muslim nations. Those countries such as Japan that did not send troops made compensating financial contributions.

By the mid-1990s, U.S. taxpayers ended up being completely reimbursed for the cost of the first gulf war. U.S. and civilian causalities were held to a minimum. The world approved of U.S. leadership, and the coalition of forces was real and broad, not cosmetic. The civilized world, Muslim and non-Muslim alike, came together to drive Saddam out of Kuwait and to establish the precedent that under international law, unprovoked attacks on his neighboring nations would be punished.

In contrast, the more recent war in Iraq has led to a devastating drop in world approval of the United States and sharp divisions between the Muslim and non-Muslim communities. It has provided more recruits for anti-American terrorist organizations, cost American taxpayers billions of dollars, and above all, caused loss of human life on a tragically large scale. A failure to understand the culture and history of other parts of the world has exacted a great price. Winston Churchill, writing to then–British prime minister David Lloyd George in 1922, prophetically described Britain's attempt to occupy Iraq as "living on a . . . volcano" without any beneficial results.[2]

The Middle East is not the only area of strategic importance to the United States. As we live through the first decade of the twenty-first century, it is clear that Asia will have increased power and influence with each passing year. If we do not know and understand Chinese history, for example, we could make unintentional blunders that could threaten our security. Unless we know about the Cultural Revolution of the 1960s in China, we cannot understand why the massacre of the students in Tiananmen Square took place. During that earlier tumultuous period, roving and unpredictable gangs known as Red Guards terrorized the country, seizing power from party leaders, pushing them from their homes, closing universities, and destroying historical monuments. Family members of future Chinese leaders were injured or killed. Deng Xiaoping's own son, Deng Pufang, was forced out of a fourth-story window by Red

Guards and left a paraplegic. Those who have suffered from disorder put a high priority on order that others might find hard to understand.

Unless we understand the history of colonial rule in China, which led to events like the Boxer Rebellion, we cannot understand the depth of Chinese nationalism. A nation whose people have been forced to live under the police forces of other countries and have had their guilt or innocence assessed by foreign courts under foreign law understandably had strong feelings about reclaiming Hong Kong from British colonial rule.

Events in China's colonial past explain the real danger that China may react with massive force if Taiwan tries to assert its separate legal independence, even though China has for several years tolerated Taiwan's de facto autonomy. Today's generation of American policy makers must be steeped in the history of critical areas of the world. Iraq is but one example of what can result from a lack of historical and cultural knowledge. We cannot afford the toll that multiple Iraq-like mistakes would take on America, especially as we deal with emerging nations whose power and influence will become great as time passes.

We must realize that we live in a world rapidly becoming multipolar. If economic trends continue, nations such as China and India, which each have five times our population, will soon have economies as large as our own. As the European Union shows signs of becoming more integrated, it will also become increasingly independent of the United States and will often go its own way.

Does this mean that America's influence in the world and our security and well-being at home will be greatly diminished in this century? Are the pessimists right? I certainly don't think so. But we need to prepare to play our role in a different way. Although the world is not yet multipolar, with several superpowers, it soon will be. We must prepare now for that development.

Two of my heroes were both British prime ministers—Winston Churchill and Harold Macmillan. I admire them for very different reasons. Churchill's moral courage is clear for all to see. He stood alone and sacrificed his own political career to fight against appeasement and prepare to defend against Hitler's aggression. Without Churchill, World War II might have ended very differently. Although Macmillan is often overshadowed by his more charismatic predecessor, it was he who had the foresight to tell the British people after World War II that the days of the empire were behind them. He educated his own people so that they could continue to play a meaningful role in world affairs but in a very different way. His most famous declaration of these ideas came in what has become known as "The Wind of Change" speech, delivered to the South African Parliament in 1960.[3] "The wind of change is blowing," Macmillan said. "We must all accept it as a fact, and our national policies must take account of it." Notwithstanding the dramatic reduction of Britain's economic power in the world and of its military standing, he argued, British values, often shared with America, could continue to influence the world. Macmillan worked hard to maintain voluntary partnerships among the nations that had once been British colonies. He also understood that the diplomatic skills developed over many years could be of great benefit to Britain and its allies in the Cold War. Certainly Britain today, with its skill and experience in diplomacy, still plays a far larger role in world affairs than its population, gross domestic product, or military strength would indicate.

As Americans we certainly do not face a change of position as dramatic as that which Britain faced in the decade following World War II. For decades to come, we are likely to be the strongest nation in the world both militarily and economically. We will wield considerable influence around the globe, but we need leaders who have the courage to tell us that we will not be able to dominate the world. Indeed, if we want to enhance our influence, we should not seek domination.

We should begin by placing as much emphasis on building our nonmilitary strength as we have placed on building military might. This does not mean that we should ever neglect our military strength. We should do all that is possible to remain the strongest nation in the world militarily, and we must always be prepared to use that military power if necessary.

At the same time, when faced with challenges, we should view a military response as a last resort. We need to sharpen and hone our diplomatic strengths. Joseph Nye in his book *The Paradox of American Power* makes the point that while we have never been so militarily superior, we have also never been so dependent on the rest of the world. We need to build new institutions that will nurture our alliances and partnerships.

The alliance that existed at the end of the first Persian Gulf War, for example, involved virtually all the major nations in the world, including many Muslim nations. After the fighting ended, nothing was done to institutionalize that alliance and focus it on other challenges such as the spread of weapons of mass destruction or the spread of terrorism. Without institutionalization, the alliance quickly vanished.

We need to clearly express and advocate our basic values of freedom, democracy, and human rights and continue to inspire the rest of the world by our actions. Business corporations now realize that damage to their reputations can dramatically affect profits. As the nation that works hardest to convert the world to our values, we must recognize how quickly others seize upon any perceived hypocrisy on our part. The events at Abu Ghraib and Guantánamo may not be major domestic political issues, but Americans need to understand how dramatically they undermine our moral influence in the rest of the world.

The twenty-first century can be remembered as the "Second American Century" if we shoulder our responsibility to develop a coherent blueprint as well as the World War II generation shouldered theirs. Several major elements that should be part of the plan are becoming increasingly clear.

First, we must begin by better understanding the rest of the world. Only by understanding the culture and history of others can we project the kind of respect and understanding on which lasting partnerships are based. Each year more than 500,000 students from around the world have come to this country to study at American colleges and universities. Their presence here has brought enormous benefits. It helps the United States maintain its leadership in higher education and research, which is critical to our long-term economic strength. Above all, it means that many of the world's future leaders will have lived in the United States. The vast majority of those who return to their home countries take with them a better understanding of our political system and our society. They become some of America's strongest friends and advocates around the world. Recent policies that make it more difficult for international students to obtain student visas urgently need to be reversed. Other countries have already begun aggressively recruiting international students alienated by what appears to be an unwelcoming attitude on the part of the American government.

While it is extremely important for international students to continue to come here to learn about us, it is just as important that more American students have experiences studying and working through internships in other countries. Historically the number of American students who study abroad has been only one-third or less the number of international students who come here. Of those American students, 90 percent have studied in Britain, France, Germany, Spain, or Italy. More students come to the United States from Malaysia alone each year than there are American students studying in all the rest of the world outside those few European countries.

Almost no Americans study in those vast areas of

the world increasingly important to our future. We are not learning about their cultures, languages, or history. In the past decade, under the National Security Education Program, more than 3,000 American students have received undergraduate or graduate scholarships to study in non-European nations in return for a commitment to government service once their studies are completed. We should be sending many times that number. Our ability to build constructive partnerships crucial to our national security depends on our understanding of others based on education and shared experiences. American universities urgently need to place more emphasis on the teaching of foreign languages and international and area studies.

The Cold War brought many countries together with us to work for a common goal. With this external threat now removed, a second major element of our blueprint must be to consciously seek other common goals that unite us with other nations. Sharing experiences and working together for a common purpose create binding ties of friendship. Prince Hassan bin Talal of Jordan has wisely suggested that we create an International Peace Corps modeled on the successful American Peace Corps. This initiative could be another valuable part of a new foreign-policy blueprint. Bringing young people together to work on worthwhile projects holds great promise for creating a network of responsible world leaders and citizens. While the United States should play a leading role in creating such an organization, all participating nations should share in developing its policies and projects. An International Peace Corps would provide a prime opportunity for us to learn from others and to listen to their points of view.

Third, when it comes to understanding the rest of the world, we must make sure that our intelligence system provides the best possible information for our policy makers, including the president. In many ways we live in a world overwhelmed by information. The late historian Daniel Boorstin expressed his concern that the sheer volume of information available to us through technological advances might make us less wise and less well educated. He recognized that information is not identical to knowledge.

During the six years I chaired the Intelligence Committee of the U.S. Senate, the volume of information flowing into the Central Intelligence Agency (CIA) increased exponentially. Satellites and other national technical capabilities created an avalanche of data. The volume of data often overwhelmed the ability of human analysts to separate the important from the unimportant.

Each day, the president is given a briefing paper of a few short pages compiled by the CIA and other intelligence agencies. It distinguishes immediate from longer-term challenges. The wisdom of a president's actions is often influenced by the quality of the analysis of information.

For decades our intelligence community focused on the Soviet threat. The agencies were organized to penetrate large nation-state organizations, to track military movements and developments, and to predict the decisions of highly centralized power structures. Our intelligence agencies focused less well on broad economic trends and on ethnic tensions and religious divisions and the threats that might stem from them. We tended to know more about what went on in competing military and intelligence organizations than we knew about public opinion on the streets of the Middle East, for example.

In addition, organizations, especially those that operate under a cloak of secrecy, tend over time to become inbred and inward looking and to define national security threats in narrower terms. Information is often "stovepiped," that is, not shared with experts in other disciplines. Information often arrives on the desks of policy makers that tells them what they want to hear, not what they need to hear. To be sure, there are debates, sometimes heated, between analysts and operatives within the intelligence community, but they tend to be more constrained and less open than those at universities or in the journalistic community.

While I certainly do not demean either the incredible ability or heroic patriotism of those in the intelligence community, I found some of our best national experts among academic scholars, business leaders operating worldwide, and journalists posted in other countries. They hesitate to become identified as intelligence operatives or to join CIA-like intelligence organizations even for a brief time. At the same time, our president and policy makers need the expertise of these keen observers and their independent thinking. It is time to create an independent government think tank through which those Americans who are not affiliated with intelligence organizations can share their expertise and observations with policy makers without having their independence compromised. Creating such an institution could help our leaders take a broader, longer-range view of our national security challenges.

Environmental policy is a fourth area of importance to improving our tattered relations with other nations. By 2012 the international community will again face the question of devising shared environmental standards. The failure of the United States, China, and India to approve the Kyoto accords left the impression with other countries that we are not willing to join with them in dealing responsibly with environmental problems. It is impossible to ignore the stress on our planet caused by the rapid growth of world population in the last century. It took 10,000 generations for world populations to reach 2 billion people. In the span of a single generation—ours—the population has increased from 2 billion to 6.5 billion and is on its way to 9 billion by the midpoint of this century.[4]

Our perceived failure to lead and to cooperate with the rest of the world in meeting the environmental challenge has also contributed to negative attitudes toward the United States. It is vitally important that the United States be prepared to offer reasonable proposals during the next round of decisions that will follow the Kyoto agreements.

Working together with China and India as well as with Europe will be crucial. We should already be actively engaged in the task. Once reasonable limits are placed on carbon and greenhouse gas emissions, we need to help make change affordable without creating huge economic dislocations and job losses in the United States and the fastest-developing nations. We need to provide financial incentives for the creation of new jobs related to a cleaner environment. In addition, we have the opportunity to convince others to join us in creating new institutions based on market forces that will keep the economic costs for all of us as low as possible. The model already exists at the Chicago Climate Exchange, where emissions credits can be traded and sold to those who need to reduce emissions. For example, if it is less expensive for one company to reduce emissions than it is for another company, the first company can take action and sell credits to the other. The atmosphere receives the same benefit, but in a more cost-effective way. This model of a voluntary but legally binding commitment to reduce greenhouse gases in the absence of the federal government taking action might be extended to other pollutants or to such scarce public goods as water. The private sector as well as state and local governments can achieve many objectives in the absence of national policy. The model might also be extended to sovereign nations not committed to reduce emissions under an international treaty.

Fifth, the most important element needed to create a New World Order is the creation of a standing military force composed of leading nations to deal with international emergencies and enforce the work of international weapons inspections. This idea is not new. President Truman, addressing the UN General Assembly in October 1946, said, "We shall press for the preparation of agreements in order that the Security Council

may have at its disposal peace forces adequate to prevent acts of aggression." Article 43 of the United Nations charter provides for nations to designate specific
military units to train and work together with those in
other countries. No nation would give up its own sover-
eignty. American troops, for example, would be committed to combat only if the American Congress and
president made that decision under our Constitution.

The promise of such a force was never realized because of the Cold War and the Soviet Union's use of its
veto power in the UN Security Council. However, with
the end of the Cold War, there is now the opportunity
to create such a force. The United States cannot afford
to stand alone as the policeman of the world. We no
longer have the economic resources to bear that burden. Above all, we should not follow policies that place
the lives of young Americans at risk without that risk
being shared with other countries. Such a force could
be created within the United Nations or, if more practical, established by consenting nations in a separate organization. Then-president George H. W. Bush, spoke
about such a possibility at the end of the first Persian
Gulf War and even mentioned Fort Dix, then scheduled
for closing, as a possible location for training an international force. Up to 100,000 troops could have been
trained and equipped for rapid deployment. Members
of the broad coalition that fought to oust Saddam Hussein from Kuwait could have been original members if
we had taken the lead at the time to make the coalition
permanent.

Efforts to create ad hoc international forces that

have no permanence often fail. In Somalia in the early 1990s, for example, a UN force struggled to end the widespread starvation caused by the fighting between warring political factions. On an inspection tour of the region, I saw firsthand why the UN effort had failed and American forces eventually had to be withdrawn. The troops from different nations had to work with incompatible equipment, hampering communication even between units. These units had never trained together. Their leaders did not know each other. They had different rules of engagement for dealing with threatening military situations and violent civilian rioting.

The building of a joint force trained together to form a working relationship long before any crisis develops would do much to make the world a safer place. It would help discourage regional conflicts, violations of basic justice, and the proliferation of weapons and international terrorism.

As we face an extended fight against terrorism around the world, building effective multinational forces will be even more essential. In addition, a structure must be established to bring together on a regular basis intelligence experts from nations threatened by terrorism. After 9/11, we acted swiftly and effectively against Al Qaeda in Afghanistan and elsewhere, largely because of vital intelligence shared with us by friendly national intelligence services. A network for constant intelligence sharing needs to be established with other nations just as we work to more completely integrate the information collected by our own CIA and FBI.

Along with a standing international military force,

an international inspection team to deal with the threats posed by terrorist cells, criminal groups, and the spread of weapons of mass destruction should also be developed. Common rules would have to be agreed upon for on-site inspections. To provide moral leadership, the United States would have to be prepared to accept the same levels of inspection for its own programs as would reasonably be required of other nations. We already have an example of international cooperation in this area in the Nunn-Lugar Agreement with the Soviet Union, designed to reduce the spread of nuclear weapons.

In addition, dealing with the terrorist threat through military action alone is like treating the symptoms of a disease without attacking the disease itself. Some degree of order must be achieved before we can deal with the underlying causes that enable fanatical terrorist leaders to recruit followers. Economic need and frustrated ethnic dreams of self-determination must ultimately be addressed, as the Marshall Plan addressed conditions that, left unattended, could have made communism and Soviet leadership far more attractive in Western Europe at the end of World War II.

While multinational military forces are important, we must remember that many of the problems we face do not lend themselves to purely military solutions. Preemptive military engagements in the absence of an act of war against us have not proven successful. Vietnam and Iraq are dramatic examples. The war on terrorism would be more accurately called the campaign against terrorism since, although some military action may be needed, it is only one component of a broad effort to win the hearts and minds of world populations. Multilateral institutions designed to act in a comprehensive way are needed.

The creation of these new institutions will not be easy. We may not find the United Nations able or willing to participate in all of these new institutions. If we cannot create them under the umbrella of the United Nations—and I hope we can—we must be prepared to create separate international organizations, just as we did when we first created NATO. (NATO peacekeeping forces have been relatively successful.) Tremendous time and energy will have to be expended. Perfection will not be achieved, but the effort to design a new blueprint must begin. Our current incoherent, ad hoc approach to foreign policy is not sustainable.

The redefinition of America's role in the world is not an issue that should be confined to Rhodes Scholarship interviews. It should rise to the top of the national agenda to be discussed by all of us.

At the end of World War II, Americans met the moral and intellectual challenges facing them. History has judged them favorably. What will be written about this generation remains to be determined.

CHAPTER TWO

The Destructiveness of Partisanship

From the earliest periods of our nation's history, thoughtful leaders have worried about the dangers posed by political parties or factions. George Washington often expressed his fear that factions would prevent Americans from coming together to take crucial action. He viewed the rise of political parties with alarm. James Madison wrote in the Federalist Papers about the need to prevent any one political faction from achieving dominance.

Over the years, Americans have come to accept political parties and the competition between them as both inevitable and to some degree healthy. While competition has its benefits and can lead to more accountability and better performance, partisanship clearly becomes destructive when partisan advantage is elevated above the national interest. That is exactly what has happened in recent years. The American people are rightly fed up with the situation but feel helpless to change it. Poll after poll indicates that the people are not satisfied with the choices the two major political parties have provided in recent presidential elections. At times half or more of those polled have expressed the need for another political organization that would unite the country. Those who describe themselves as moderates make up a large part of both existing parties but feel more and more disenfranchised by the extreme polar elements of each. John Zogby recently wrote about the results his polling organization found: "The middle ground of the political electorate is expanding, and the fringes are contracting across the political spectrum. There is widespread dissatisfaction with where America is headed right now!" He pointed to his polling data indicating that 80 percent of Americans believe that it is "very important" that the next president be a person who can unite the country. Another 58 percent said that it was "very important" that the next president cross party lines to work with political opponents. Another recent survey found that 83 percent of Americans believe that the nation is so polarized between Democrats and Republicans that Washington can't make progress in solving major problems. Americans desire viable choices, but the current state of affairs reminds me of what Harvard political scientist V. O. Key wrote about the two-party system in his 1966 book, *The Responsible Electorate:* "Given the choice between scoundrels, the electorate will likely pick one." Seventy-three percent of Americans recently polled felt that it would be good to have choices in the next presidential election in addition to the Republican and Democratic nominees.[1]

At a time when Americans urgently need to come together to act decisively at home and abroad, partisan bickering has paralyzed our ability to act. For example, it is long past time to bring our budget deficits under control and to contain the costs of entitlement programs such as Social Security and Medicare. Many of the solutions are obvious, but each party is afraid to act because of the attacks they know will come from the other side to artfully press the emotional hot buttons of American voters.

Specific solutions to foreign policy crises like those in the Middle East get delayed for fear that normal diplomatic dialogue, even with nations that are not our allies, will be portrayed as weakness or being soft on terrorism. Long gone is the wise agreement that "politics should stop at the water's edge" when it comes to international matters so that the United States can speak with a single voice. Now romanticized as irretrievably lost are the times when members of Congress had strong personal friendships across party lines. We are told that we cannot recreate the days when Democratic Senate leader Lyndon Johnson and Republican leader Everett Dirksen could sit down over dinner after a heated public debate and meet each other halfway to strike an agreement on the most controversial issues of the day.

No fundamental obstacle prevents the spirit of bipartisanship that brought the United States to world leadership in the twentieth century from being recreated. It must be done. As citizens we must insist on it by punishing at the ballot box those who shun bipartisan cooperation.

We must recall how constructive bipartisan cooperation can be. Think about what was accomplished in the immediate aftermath of World War II. The blueprint that brought us victory in the Cold War and sustained us for more than four decades could never have been put together without bipartisan cooperation. Year after year, these solid policies were consistently followed under presidents and Congresses of both political parties.

Imagine how easily the Republicans in Congress could have scuttled the Marshall Plan proposed by President Truman, General George C. Marshall, and Secretary of State Dean Acheson. If today's partisanship had been present in the late 1940s, the Republican opposition would have been running ads saying, "The Democrats want to tax you to help the very people who killed and wounded our fathers and sons, who threatened our security and brought us economic hardship." It doesn't take much imagination to predict what the result would have been. Perhaps they would have added, "Bring our boys home. Why keep troops in Europe now that the war is over? Let Europeans defend themselves against the Russians."

Instead, great bipartisan leaders such as Arthur Vandenberg of Michigan, Republican leader of the Senate Foreign Relations Committee, joined Democrats in supporting the Marshall Plan and the policy of containment. He and others passed up the opportunity to score cheap shots against the party in power and, instead, put the national interest first. Bipartisan statesmanship by leaders of both parties brought America to leadership abroad and progress at home, with a doubling of real incomes for Americans in less than thirty years. This progress came because of increases in productivity produced by such programs as the GI Bill, which made the American workforce the best educated in the world.

How have we come to lose that spirit of bipartisanship on crucial matters? Why do so many politicians no longer feel an obligation to act responsibly and to reject purely partisan agendas when the national interest is at stake? There are several reasons.

The principal cause of the demise of bipartisanship is the way in which we finance campaigns. I return to that issue later, but suffice it to say here that the cost of being elected today bears no resemblance to the cost of campaigns even twenty, let alone fifty, years ago. The money comes more and more from groups with single-issue agendas as opposed to the broad national interest. Loyalty to party leaders and party agendas also drives an increasingly large part of the distribution of campaign funds.

Slowly but surely, we have institutionalized partisanship. When I first came to the U.S. Senate in 1979, there was an unwritten tradition that a sitting senator never campaigned against a senator who was up for reelection, even if he or she was of the opposing party. When I left the Senate in 1994, I may have been the last remaining senator to have still followed that unwritten policy known as the Mansfield Rule. It was named for Democratic Senate leader Mike Mansfield, who had urged this policy of bipartisanship for many years. As the tradition disintegrated, I sometimes observed senators from one party taking notes about votes that could be used against senators of the other party in attack ads during campaigns. I remember the day when a senator sitting next to me in a committee meeting said that our colleague on the committee from the other party had a good amendment but that he was going to vote against it. "Why?" I asked. "Because," he replied, "the SOB came to my state and campaigned against me and lied about me, and I'll never support anything he proposes."

Party caucuses did not meet very regularly until the 1960s and 1970s. Earlier, senators of the same party met alone together only a few times each year. Then the meetings became monthly. By the time I arrived in Washington, the meetings were weekly. Each week, all of the Republicans met in a separate room together and had lunch and a three-hour discussion. The Democrats did the same. Nearly always, the topic was how we could force the members of the opposing party to vote on a proposal that would make them look like they were against education, or family values, or national defense. Almost none of the caucus luncheon discussions had to do with serving the national interest. The talk was all about positioning to win the next election. Dissenters who wanted to seek a bipartisan agreement with the other party were subjected to peer pressure to be more loyal to the party. In the House of Representatives, there was even greater pressure, and committee assignments or chairmanships were put at risk if the party line was not followed.

No equivalent institution existed to encourage bipartisanship. No regular bipartisan caucuses met in which moderates of both parties could work together to fashion an American approach to issues.

What a contrast the current political climate presents with what I experienced earlier in my Senate career. I recall a day when the Senate was voting on a proposal to change the tax law as it applied to horses. Senator Max Baucus of Montana and I, both Democrats and both freshmen, had misunderstood the proposal and had voted against the interest of our states on the roll call. Before the vote was closed, a senior Republican from Tennessee, Senator Howard Baker, came over and explained the proposal to us. Since we were from "horse-raising states," he told us, he thought we would want to change our votes. We did. Today, you would rarely if ever see a senior member of one party helping freshman members of the other party avoid political mistakes. In addition, no longer do new senators or representatives of different parties become well acquainted and form personal friendships. The dozen new senators who came to the U.S. Senate when I did in January of 1979 all became close friends. Half of us were Democrats and half were Republicans. We regularly enjoyed pot-luck dinners at one anothers' homes with our spouses. Party differences never interfered with our friendships or kept us from working together.

Because redistricting fashioned by increasingly partisan state legislatures has reduced the number of truly competitive House districts, party leaders and partisanship have grown even stronger. Party leaders are able to dominate other members. The distribution of party-controlled money has added to the trend. Each year, more and more moderates voluntarily or involuntarily leave Congress.

Soon after I first arrived in the Senate in 1979, Howard Baker said to me, "Remember it is those who play between the forty-yard lines [the moderates] who really determine the outcome of the contest." At that time at least one-fourth, perhaps one-third, of senators potentially belonged to that middle group. Today the number has shrunk to four or five senators in each party out of one hundred.[2]

In earlier years, and especially during the Cold War, it was not unusual for congressional leaders of both parties to meet with the president and key cabinet officers to work out real policy decisions. These meetings have become rare and have largely turned into photo ops aimed at creating a public relations image of bipartisanship instead of the real thing.

We all remember the scene on the Capitol steps shortly after the terrorist attacks of 9/11. Prominent congressional leaders of both parties locked arms and sang "God Bless America." It was a wonderful moment. If only it could have continued! The bipartisan spirit lasted barely a week. What can be done to create more true bipartisanship and to reverse the relentless march toward destructive partisanship?

There are no easy answers. But the difficult answers can be identified. First, a major answer is campaign finance reform. More of the financial resources for candidates need to come from individual contributors in a candidate's home state. These home-state voters and contributors can evaluate members of Congress according to their total record of service instead of on the basis of a few votes important to special-interest groups. The framers of our Constitution intended for members of Congress to represent the citizens of their home states and districts, not well-financed special-interest groups that may have little connection to those home constituencies.

Second, as we struggle to create bipartisanship, we must seek to create institutions that encourage it. If after 9/11 President George W. Bush had created real joint executive-congressional working groups that met frequently, the bipartisanship symbolized by the locking of arms on the Capitol steps might have lasted.

We have learned that when presidential administrations develop major policies without real input from the opposition party in Congress, a predictable partisan reaction results, followed by open political warfare and gridlock. It would be worth trying to institutionalize regular behind-closed-door meetings of standing bipartisan working groups that would include the key legislative and executive branch leaders in two or three key fields. One of these joint "mini-cabinets" might be in the field of foreign policy and national security. It would include not only the president but also the secretaries of state and defense and the national security adviser. It could include the ranking Democrats and Republicans in the House and Senate committees on Foreign Relations, Armed Services, and Intelligence. A similar group might be formed on domestic economic issues. These groups could meet regularly to try to hammer out consensus proposals. It is always easier to compromise behind closed doors before major presidential proposals are made than to do so after they are made public and battle lines have been drawn.

Third, after 9/11, I believe that a bipartisan program for major public works and infrastructure investment could have been agreed upon if the leaders of both parties had met together at that time. We have been under-investing in basic infrastructure for many years. Needed infrastructure investments could have created jobs in the aftermath of the terrorist attacks and helped prevent the economic slowdown that followed.

Of course, there will never be full agreement on all major issues, and our political system would not be healthy if there were. However, we must at least attempt to find new ways and new institutions that will make more likely the formation of a consensus on how to deal with the major challenges that threaten our national well-being. It is even worth trying to encourage moderates in both parties to form a bipartisan caucus that meets regularly to act as an antidote to purely partisan caucuses. Perhaps it is too much to hope that the leaders of both parties in both houses would urge members to reinstate the practice of not campaigning against each other. The leaders will do so only if they feel they will be rewarded in the court of public opinion.

Finally, if the cycle of ever increasing partisanship is not reversed, we should elect an independent president who comes from neither party. That president could pledge to form a national unity cabinet composed of the best-qualified men and women in both parties, much like Churchill's "war cabinet" during World War II. The use of joint legislative-executive branch working groups might enable an independent president to govern effectively for at least a limited time.

I hope that an independent would serve as president without forming a new third party. It is not necessary in any of the fifty states to form a new party in order to place a candidate on the ballot. An independent candidate may be placed on the ballot in all states, with a vice presidential candidate of his or her selection, by collecting fewer than 900,000 signatures on petitions nationwide. In most states, a three-month period opens as early as March 1 during which petitions must be circulated. It is thus possible for an independent presidential candidate to run and be elected, but the process could be made much easier through ballot reform.

The two-party system has proven largely beneficial. It should not be discarded lightly to be replaced by a multiparty system. One need only look at the chaotic multiparty democracies in Western Europe to know that there are potential pitfalls. Perhaps a brief time-out from the two-party patterns with an effective independent president would create forces for greater bipartisanship in the future. After four or eight years of working together with an independent president in a unity government, it would, one would hope, be possible for us to return to our historic two-party system while avoiding the destructive partisanship of the last few years.

One thing is clear: public impatience with partisan bickering has reached the boiling point. It is feeding the cynicism Americans feel about their own government. It is tragically contributing to the sense of pessimism about the future of our country and the quality of life for our children. We must break the cycle of partisanship or face inevitable decline as a nation.

As Americans work to reawaken the spirit of bipartisanship, we also need to strive to change the tone of public debate. Political talk shows have become shouting matches designed to push emotional hot buttons and drive us further apart. Instead, we desperately need to exchange ideas with one another rationally and courteously. We need to concentrate on the values we share as Americans around which we can unite as a people. Above all, our society would benefit from a healthy infusion of old-fashioned kindness and courtesy. There is a quiet power in kindness. The way we treat each other will help determine the kind of society we will pass on to our children.

CHAPTER THREE

Campaign Corruption

Few would dispute that our Constitution is indispensable to the continuation of our political system and to the preservation of our individual rights. At the same time, history has shown that written documents alone cannot preserve freedom. The written constitution of Weimar Germany did not prevent the rise of Hitler and his manipulation of major institutions to enhance his power. The constitution of the former Soviet Union appeared democratic on its face, but clearly it functioned only as a cover for the dictatorship of the Communist Party and its leaders. While Britain has the Magna Carta, it has no detailed written constitution. Yet it has retained a stable, free, and democratic society for centuries through legal precedents in the courts and the strong devotion to the individual freedom of its people. The values we tenaciously hold and the respect for the rights of others that we embrace in our hearts provide the real protection for our political system. If we stop caring about our constitutional system and become alienated from it, the written document will not preserve itself.

That is why the growing cynicism of the American people about their own government is so alarming. When we stop believing we can make a difference by participating in politics, the future of our system is at risk. Yet as I indicated earlier in this letter, the polling data show exactly that trend.

Every time I teach the students in my political science class, I keep in mind that the polls indicate that about 80 percent of them no longer believe that the government cares about people like them or truly represents their views. More than three-fourths of them don't believe our leaders will usually do the right thing. The stark difference between current American attitudes toward government and those of my own student days continues to frighten me.

This high level of cynicism does not mean that this generation of students simply doesn't care about the future or about helping others. Volunteer service is on the rise again after three decades of decline, and the largest increase in giving back is coming from young people twenty-five years of age and under. This generation wants to make a difference. For the most part, they try to treat each other with kindness and respect. They want to be good parents one day. They realize that some of the trade-offs often required for material success are not worth the costs. To cite one reason for my optimism about America's future, I have confidence in the values of this current generation of college and university students. Yet this student generation is cynical about its own government and cynical about politics in general. I want them to share my optimism about our future and my deep feelings of pride in the genius and fairness of our political system.

Not long ago, a prominent Washington journalist

came to visit with some of our outstanding students. Like me, she had been influenced by the call of such leaders as President John F. Kennedy to enter the political arena and make a difference. "How many of you plan to run for office someday?" she asked a group of about one hundred students. Almost no hands went up. Thinking she had been misunderstood, she asked again, "I mean how many of you think you might want to be a governor, congressman, U.S. senator, or even president some day?" Still virtually no hands were raised. She looked at me with a confused and upset expression. Finally she blurted out, "Don't any of you even care about what is going to happen to your country?"

At that point I intervened. I asked a different series of questions. "How many of you plan to be active in a religious organization?" Many hands went up. "How many of you plan to be active in charitable organizations and perhaps serve as officers of nonprofit groups?" Again most hands went up. "How many of you might consider serving on your local school board or as leaders of your neighborhood association?" A majority of the hands went up. I was not surprised by the results, but it was fascinating to watch her reaction. Those who live in Washington tend to believe that most people in America are very interested in what goes on there and feel very involved in it. In fact, most Americans, including my students, don't feel that what goes on there is particularly relevant to their lives. Nor do they feel they can have much impact on what happens there.

This disconnect between Washington and the people was very surprising to me when I quit the U.S. Senate to come home to be an educator. Even though throughout my Senate career I returned to Oklahoma at least forty times a year to hold meetings with my constituents, I later realized that I had been living in an artificial environment. The people who came to meetings were among the small percentage who were still involved in politics. Because I was a senator, people tended to be less candid with me.

After returning home, I found that I too was much more interested in what was happening in my community and in the lives of my students than I was in the political activities in which I had invested twenty-eight years of my life. I'm certainly not suggesting that involvement in things close at hand is not healthy. What concerns me is that most Americans, including my students, do not believe that what is going on in national politics has much to do with them. Even worse, they feel powerless to change what they do not like. I cannot help but believe that this cynicism about politics, which is far above historic norms, is a major reason why Americans now believe that our future will not be as great as our past.

The bonds of trust between the people and their government and the belief that grassroots democracy really works are critically important. These beliefs helped bring us through several crises like the Great Depression without weakening our political system. The Great Depression helped bring Hitler to power in Germany, but in the United States our system survived. The voters turned to Franklin D. Roosevelt, who sought to preserve the system, and overwhelmingly rejected fringe figures with revolutionary agendas. Americans had faith in their system and felt they could get things done by participating in politics.[1] How well would we weather such a crisis today?

Why does this cynicism exist? Early in each semester I seek to find out from my students. When I ask questions, the same answers always come back. "Politics today is all about money." "Those with the most money win the elections." "The money doesn't come from people like us, but from political action committees and lobbyists." One said blatantly, "I don't have any say in government, because I don't have enough money to buy a congressman."

Even though I anticipate their answers, it hurts to hear them. Many people living today were influenced by President Kennedy to enter politics because it was seen as a way to make a difference. We wanted to make the country better than we had found it, and we viewed involvement in politics as the best way to accomplish that objective. To hear the perceptions of a role I had played for twenty-eight years described in such cynical and negative terms by this generation of students is painful. Recently a freshman at the university came up to me and said that he wanted to visit with me because, he said, "I used to want to go into politics, but now I don't think anyone can make a difference by doing that."

It was as painful to me as the comment made by the wife of the Soviet ambassador at a dinner party in Washington. She was a hard-line communist not known for graciousness. "Your government is no more democratic than ours," she said to me. "Whoever has the most money always wins the elections. You're all bought and paid for," she concluded.

Even a quick look at what is happening to the cost of campaigns explains why these negative perceptions exist and reveals them to be right on target. While the cost of campaigns has been a problem for many years, it has exploded recently to heights not even comparable to prior periods. In 1976, when Gerald Ford and Jimmy Carter faced off in the presidential election, they spent a combined $67 million. George W. Bush and Al Gore spent $343 million in 2000. By 2004 the funds directly spent by George W. Bush and John Kerry had doubled to $718 million. By July 2007, with fifteen months remaining before the next presidential election, the candidates had already raised $265 million. Clearly, we are on a path to doubling the costs every four years. It would not be surprising during the current election cycle to see presidential candidates spend more on their campaigns than the National Cancer Institute will spend in 2007 to fight the four most deadly forms of that disease.

Running for Congress has also never been so expensive. In 1974, spending for all House candidates totaled $44 million, averaging $53,000 per candidate. By 2004, the figure had reached $581 million, with candidates averaging $773,000. The Senate races cost a combined $28 million in 1974, jumping to $367 million in 2004, with the average spending for each candidate moving from $437,000 to $5.4 million.[2]

A major part of increased campaign costs is spending on television advertising. It is not unusual for a U.S. Senate candidate to spend $1 million or more on thirty-second television spots for a single week during a campaign.

The cost of television advertising is further increased by the length of campaigns. In many countries in Europe, for example, campaigning is allowed only during a limited period of sixty or ninety days. It is illegal to spend money for media advertising, signs, or direct mail except during that period. In our own country, campaigns are now so long that the time between them is getting shorter than the campaigns themselves. In some countries, television time is allocated free in equal amounts to party nominees, and they are required to use it in longer time blocks in order to truly inform the voters instead of using television for emotional thirty-second attack spots. The airwaves belong to the public, and Congress can therefore take positive steps to regulate them in ways that enhance the political process.

The problem is not only that too much additional money is going into campaigns but also that it is coming from the wrong places. Many members of Congress receive well over half of their campaign contributions from special-interest political action committees (PACs) and donors located outside home states and districts. It is no wonder that the perception is growing that money, not merit, is determining political outcomes. The basic concept of grassroots democracy is inevitably eroded when candidates can win with money from people who have never even set foot inside the home states or districts of senators and representatives.

In recent years, a system already awash in special-interest cash has been further corrupted by members of

Congress who set up their own PACs to dole out money to one another. They do so to win leadership positions and key committee assignments within Congress. In 1998 there were 120 of these so-called leadership political action committees, and they gave out $11 million to fellow members. By 2006 there were 285 such PACs giving out almost $42 million. Members of Congress are "taxed" to raise money for their leaders' PACs. Those who raise money for this purpose are rewarded with chairmanships, good committee assignments, and other positions of power inside Congress.[3]

Leadership PACs are also established to evade campaign contribution limits. An individual can contribute only $4,600 to a candidate for each entire election cycle; but instead of giving $4,600, the same person can give $5,000 per year or $30,000 to a senator's leadership PAC. Because they are separate from campaign committees, the PACs can also use funds for what are essentially personal expenses for these officials. One congressman paid his wife a commission of $180,000 on funds raised for his PAC. Her "consulting firm" operated from their home and had no employees, no separate telephone number, and no other clients.[4] Informed citizens, including college students, read or hear about PAC spending. It is no wonder that in one recent poll, only 14 percent of those responding believed that Congress represented people like them. How long will we wait to act? Until the figure falls to zero?

While the American people have a general feeling that money has too much influence in politics, this feeling would be even stronger if we were able to monitor carefully how it distorts the political agenda. The largest campaign contributors often represent single-issue groups or financial interest groups that make up a small percentage of the population. Yet when our leaders determine priorities for action, what gets put on the list just happens to reflect the desires of the relatively small number of people who are the biggest donors to campaigns. One politician is reported to have said, "If you want to play, you need to pay." Another said when addressing donors at a large fund-raising dinner, "I know you are here because you want good government and a whole lot more!" As Fred Wertheimer, former president of Common Cause, put it: "We must stop the practice of politicians living off their campaign money."[5]

What would we do if we woke up to newspaper banner headlines and round-the-clock cable news coverage announcing that a small group of people had taken over Congress and the White House by bribing all of our public officials? What if we were further told that all of the major decisions were being made to please that group? What if we realized that the distribution of our tax burden was determined by those who paid the bribes, and so was our foreign policy and our environmental policy and our health policy? I like to think we would march on Washington and stop it just as quickly as if we had heard that a dictator had been installed by the military and our democracy had been destroyed.

In fact, that is exactly what *has* happened. Corruption is corruption, whether it is direct or indirect. I am not suggesting that all political contributors are consciously paying bribes or that members of Congress or other public officials would accept direct payoffs. Unfortunately, the result is the same. In some ways it is more threatening than direct bribery because it is easy for the participants in the process to rationalize away what is actually going on. It is also less visible, so the public does not rise up to stop it. They would rise up if suitcases of cash were being delivered directly to buy votes. However we describe what is happening, it is preventing us from dealing with the very real problems we desperately need to face and solve.

Even those members who intentionally try to do the right thing without regard to campaign contributions come under enormous pressure from the current system of campaign finance. Because more than 90 percent of the time the candidate with the most money wins, members who want to stay in office to work for the good of the country convince themselves that they have to be practical about raising money. The typical senator needs to raise an average of $20,000 each week over an election cycle (six years) to put together a winning war chest. In large states, the figure may be ten times that much. If there is a group of people waiting to see you in your office and you have time only to see one, whom will you see? It probably won't be the college student, farmer, homemaker, teacher, small-business owner, or retail clerk. It will probably be the lobbyist who could raise $250,000 for your campaign fund at a single lunch in Washington. The member can always rationalize that if he doesn't get reelected, he cannot help the others who wanted to see him but were told that he was too busy to meet with them.

When I speak with my students and urge them to run for office, I tell them to prepare themselves, to be ready to contribute the ideas and the vision the country needs. In the backs of their minds, I know they are also asking themselves, "But how will I raise the millions of dollars I need to win the election?"

I don't know how many times I heard fellow senators bemoan the fact that they found themselves constantly on airplanes flying to fund-raisers outside their own states or districts to raise money for their reelections. Votes were sometimes scheduled on the Senate floor to accommodate out-of-town fund-raising trips. One of the results of the never ending money chase is that at a time when we face so many problems, our Congress is working for us only part-time. Senators and representatives are spending at least a third of their time raising money instead of doing what we elected them to do.

In addition, members of Congress are often in other states at fund-raisers instead of back home listening to the ideas or learning firsthand from their own constituents. Being from a relatively small state with limited financial resources, I sometimes found myself virtually forced to take time away from town meetings in my own state to go to major national financial centers to raise campaign contributions. Raising money also took important time away from the study and reflection I felt I needed to be the best possible public official.

U.S. Supreme Court decisions in cases such as *Buckley v. Valeo* have left little room for Congress to directly limit the amount that can be spent on campaigns or to regulate the source of these funds. Besides, do we really think we can trust sitting members of Congress to pass real reforms and limits on spending using the current system, which gives them a three- or four-to-one advantage in raising campaign funds over possible opponents? No one wants to offend those who are already in Congress and will be voting on their taxes or regulations of their businesses.

With each passing year, the necessity is becoming more evident to amend our Constitution to solve this problem. Since the *Buckley* case incorrectly equated the spending of unlimited amounts of campaign money with the First Amendment right of free speech, it has become almost impossible to craft a congressional bill that will pass muster with the courts. While we recognize that incumbents are usually better known than challengers, it makes sense to argue that candidates should have the ability to spend reasonable amounts of money to become known and to disseminate their views to the public. It makes no sense, however, to argue that the First Amendment requires campaign spending to be unlimited. The bankruptcy of this idea is demonstrated by the enormous campaign war chests that the already well known incumbents usually have. Unlimited spending in practice gives less than an equal chance for free speech to challengers in elections.

I joined in introducing bipartisan bills to encourage candidates to voluntarily set spending limits in return for partial government funding of campaigns and lower television advertising rates. To date, Congress has shown no appetite for raising taxes to provide these incentives or for regulating the political advertising rates of the broadcasting industry.

A constitutional amendment would free us from the limits of Supreme Court decisions, and Congress and the state legislatures could directly limit the amount spent on campaigns based on a formula reflecting the number of voters in the election. An amendment could also strengthen grassroots democracy by allowing only those who live in a candidate's home state or district to contribute to his or her campaigns. By restricting the ability to give a contribution only to those who could vote in the election, we could reduce out-of-state influences and ban all contributions from special-interest groups and political action committees. Only individuals from the home state could contribute, and total spending by the candidate could be limited, if we solve the problem through a constitutional amendment.

It is time to quit wringing our hands about too much money distorting politics and do something about it. It is time to start a national movement to draft a constitutional amendment to limit and regulate campaign spending, followed by an unstoppable effort to ratify the amendment. We may try to rationalize what is going on, but the right word for it is "corruption." If it is not stopped, it will destroy our political system.

CHAPTER FOUR

Our Economic Health

If the United States is to remain a superpower, it must be powerful economically as well as militarily.

Perhaps the greatest risk to our economy is posed by continued budget deficits that have raised the national debt, to $8.9 trillion in 2007.[1] It is very hard for us to understand this number and what it means. Some would try to pass it off as inconsequential because our gross domestic product, they argue, has grown as fast or faster than our debt. These apologists fail to take into account the political and social realities that limit our ability to deal with this debt.

A recent study by the Concord Coalition, a watchdog group of civic leaders and scholars, explained the threat in a way we can all understand it. Their most recent study indicates that if current trends continue, by the year 2020, interest on the national debt and the cost of entitlement programs such as Social Security, Medicare, and Medicaid will completely consume all the taxes we now pay. In other words, there will be no revenues left to maintain the armed forces, provide aid to education, support our transportation system, or fund our law-enforcement agencies. Obviously, we cannot do without these critical programs. We will be left to choose between huge tax increases or deep cuts in entitlement programs. Either choice has dire consequences.

To avoid that catastrophic situation, we must act now to bring down the deficit. The largest single increase in deficit spending in recent years has been the war in Iraq, which averages $9 billion per month and $100 billion per year.[2] However, even if the war is brought to a conclusion, the deficit problem will remain severe. As baby boomers reach retirement age, Social Security and Medicare spending will increase even more.

Another danger comes from high deficits. To pay the interest on the debt, the government sells bonds. More and more of the total savings of all Americans are required to make the interest payments on those bonds. For our economy to grow, Americans must be able to borrow money at a reasonable cost. Young couples need to borrow to buy homes. Businesses need to borrow to expand and create more jobs. The interest rate is the cost of borrowing money. Like anything else, the price is determined by supply and demand. If the demand for borrowing goes up faster than the supply of savings, the price or interest rate will go up. The more our government has to borrow, the more pressure is put on the interest rate. Differences in interest rates have a critical impact on economic growth. At 5 percent, the mortgage payment on a $100,000 house is a little more than $400 per month. At 10 percent, the monthly payment for the same house is more than $800. Fewer people will be able to afford to buy new houses. That means fewer jobs for carpenters, carpet layers, appliance manufacturers, and many others. High interest rates generally bring recessions and economic slowdowns. One way to avoid this problem is to increase the supply of savings to keep up with the demand fueled by government deficits. If people from other countries place their savings in the United States, it will help hold down interest rates. Over the past several years, more and more of the debt of Americans has come to be held by those in other nations. Foreigners supply more and more of the savings that Americans and our government are borrowing. But what would happen if those in other countries who hold our debt were to become angry with American policies or lose confidence in our economy and decide to place their savings elsewhere? We are placing decisions about our economic security in the hands of non-Americans. In a subtle way, we are limiting our national independence.

Finding ways to reduce entitlement spending to control deficits is not so much a question of not knowing what to do as it is a matter of political will. The solutions are not very difficult to find. Because of advances in medical sciences, we are living longer than earlier generations did, and we therefore have the ability to work longer. Older workers are often more productive because they have more experience. Raising the retirement age to qualify for Social Security and pension benefits makes sense. Likewise, age does not necessarily identify those persons with the greatest financial need. Some of our senior citizens are better off than their children, many of whom work extra jobs to pay to educate their children and meet the mortgages on the family home. Why should these younger taxpayers who are barely able to buy health insurance for themselves pay for free health insurance called Medicare for multimillionaires simply because the latter are over sixty-five years of age? Of course, that is an extreme example. Making those who are relatively well-off pay more taxes on their Social Security benefits or a greater share of their medical costs is called means testing. Highly organized groups representing people my age and older argue that allowing any means testing is the "camel's nose under the tent" and that before we know it, middle-income and even poverty-stricken senior citizens will be left without help. These groups also vote in large numbers and give generous campaign contributions. Any tinkering with entitlements is a front-line issue in the war between the political parties. Few politicians have forgotten the thirty-second television attack spot showing a tearful senior citizen looking in the mailbox for the Social Security check that is not there. Once again, we return to the need for a bipartisan truce and campaign finance reform so that sensible policy makers can fairly restructure entitlement programs to reduce the budget deficit and the dangers that come from it.

It's time to bite the bullet. The American people have sense enough to know that we cannot continue to avoid taking action. We need to substantially raise the retirement age required to draw full benefits, and we need to tax the Medicare and Social Security benefits of the wealthy who can afford to buy their own health insurance and provide for their own retirement years. Those two actions alone would do much to avert a crisis.

Education is another issue of economic importance. If we are to remain economically competitive, especially with nations that offer cheap labor, we must have the best-educated workforce in the world. The best-educated workforce will also be the most productive. It is no coincidence that the greatest single increase in economic productivity and in real incomes for Americans came in the years immediately following World War II. That is because Congress passed the GI Bill of Rights to provide free higher education for returning servicemen and -women. The GI Bill helped create the best-educated workforce in the world and the most productive.

Our educational system must strive to outperform all others. By several measures it is failing to do so. Standardized test scores indicate that among leading nations American high school students at age fifteen are outperformed in mathematics by students in twenty Organisation for Economic Co-operation and Development (OECD) countries. In other words, American students' math performance ranks in the bottom fourth among major nations.[3] Other countries also have lower dropout rates. Japan's dropout rate, for example, is less than one-fifth of ours.

An entire letter could be written about what needs to be done to improve American education, but two straightforward items come immediately to mind. First, we all know that the quality of education depends on the quality of teachers. In earlier years the United States received high quality at very low cost as generations of highly talented women went into teaching because opportunities available to them in other professions were limited. Fortunately, there are far more opportunities for women today. This also means, however, that it is increasingly difficult to attract the best and brightest into teaching.

Former Harvard president Derek Bok has thoughtfully written that the marketplace does not always reward the most important roles in our society with the highest compensation. One has only to look at salaries paid to mediocre rock stars or professional athletes as compared to inspiring teachers, social workers, and spiritual leaders to understand his thesis. There are many arguments about what should come first—higher standards for teachers or higher compensation? Why not both? One thing is clear: only major increases in compensation will attract the best and brightest teachers. Nothing could do more to improve our educational system, help our society, and strengthen our economy. We must pay teachers on the basis of their value to all of us. Sir Michael Barbor, a senior educational adviser to then–prime minister Tony Blair, recently named four great educational systems in three different continents. "What do all of the great school systems in the world all have in common?" he asked. "They all select their teachers from the top third of the college graduates, whereas the United States selects its teachers from the bottom third."[4] When we are asked to name the people who have most influenced our lives outside our own family members, most of us name teachers. Yet Americans too often begrudge paying the taxes needed to provide them adequate salaries. We should be ashamed!

Second, American students must be challenged to perform at higher levels and to work harder and longer. Let us be honest with ourselves: America's students often come to the college classroom less prepared than either their foreign peers do or their parents and grand-parents did. We must not tolerate the dumbing down of our curriculum, and we should insist that our students spend as many days in class each year as students in other countries. No wonder our students score lower on achievement tests, when they go to school each year fifteen fewer days than those in OECD (mostly European) countries and twenty-eight fewer days than students in East Asian countries. We should increase the K–12 school year by at least twenty days. During the critical years between ages five and eighteen, students in other parts of the world go to school more than the equivalent of a year longer than American students.[5]

To compete with the rest of the world economically, it is also imperative that we retain our lead in higher education and cutting-edge research. We will inevitably decline economically if we do not remain number one in creative activity, research, discovery, and the production of patents and intellectual property. Innovation is the key to what is America. In a world where manu-facturing, services, and energy production are all out-sourced, the next economic frontier for America is what has always been America's best frontier: innovation, cre-ation, and anticipation of the future. American spending on university-based research must be increased to com-pete with increases that other governments are making. We must also continue offering access to our universi-ties to the best and brightest international students and allowing many of them to remain in this country after they are trained. Over many decades some of the most talented innovators in science, technology, and other fields have been naturalized Americans who first came to the United States on student visas.

In terms of our economic strength, we also must not forget to invest in our infrastructure. On a recent visit to Spain I was struck by the quality of that country's airports and trains and the high standards of its roads. By comparison, our transportation system looks in many ways like that of a Third World country.

It is no wonder that we are falling behind. For the past three decades we have been investing only about half the percentage of our gross domestic product in infrastructure that we invested during the previous century. One of the reasons we have had improved productivity and an ability to compete in the world marketplace has been the excellence of our infrastructure. We could, for example, move agricultural products much more efficiently and less expensively from the farm gate into the world market than other countries.

As bridges collapse, dams give way, and steam tunnels break through city streets, we have come to understand that our safety, as well as our economic well-being, is tied to infrastructure investments. Our power grids need updating and protecting. We need the ability to move water from flooded areas to places where that water is desperately needed. The 2005 report card for American infrastructure estimates that it would take $1.6 trillion to bring our infrastructure in twelve different areas up to acceptable standards.[6] We should complete as soon as possible a national inventory of infrastructure needs. As funds become available, we can begin to make the needed investments. Such an inventory would also be helpful in case of a major economic slowdown like the one that occurred after 9/11. A massive public works program would have lowered unemployment and helped the economy to rebound more quickly.

We must also develop a bipartisan energy policy. The recent shock of the rise in the price of oil past $100 per barrel has awakened us to the need to act quickly to develop stronger conservation programs and new alternative energy sources. Unless we act, we will experience a huge transfer of wealth from net consuming nations like ours to other nations, some of which are not particularly friendly to the United States. The government could develop a guaranteed floor price for alternative fuels. In the past, with oil prices fluctuating to low levels from time to time, investors hesitated to make long-term commitments to alternative energy developments. With the price of oil likely to remain elevated for many years, it is unlikely that significant government costs would be related to guaranteed floor prices. We must act now on a comprehensive energy policy to protect our national security and our economic strength.

The United States will not retain its economic leadership in the world without a major effort. Even when we adopt tax policies, we must think internationally. How we tax certain products at home can affect our ability to compete in the world marketplace. No longer can we look at economic decisions as purely internal or domestic policy questions. Everything from budgetary priorities and taxes to regulatory policies affects America's international economic stature. We have sometimes been so focused on maintaining our military leadership that we have neglected our economic strength. Economic as well as moral strength will be crucial to maintaining America's position as a world leader.

CHAPTER FIVE

Our Disappearing Middle Class

Above all, America's economic health cannot be measured solely by our ability to compete with others. Our economic policies must help build a stronger society at home. Those policies must advance the basic American principle of equal opportunity for all. We must be committed to giving every child born in America an equal chance to succeed. The great strength of our country has been the middle class—the broad cross section of Americans who have worked their way through economic hard times and, without prodding, volunteered to fight for this country in times of war. They are the stockholders, the home owners, the neighborhood volunteers, and those who take the greatest responsibility for our communities.

Justice Louis Brandeis is credited with having once said, "You can have a democracy and a society sharply divided between the rich and the poor, but you cannot have both for very long."

I will never forget an evening my wife and I spent having dinner with one of the most important business leaders in Brazil. He was a jeweler with businesses around the world. At one point in our conversation he looked at me and said, "If you remember nothing else I have said tonight, I hope that you will remember my appeal to you to preserve the middle class in your country." He went on to share with me his insights into the polarization that had occurred in Brazil resulting in a small number of very wealthy people, a large group of desperately poor people, and almost no group remaining in the middle to hold the society together. While we were in Brazil, the U.S. State Department was warning Americans not to stroll along the famous Ipanema beachfront in Rio de Janeiro at night because it was not safe. Roaming groups of teenagers and even younger children had attacked and even killed tourists to steal their $20 plastic Swatch watches. Our host said to me plaintively, "What good is my wealth if I can't even walk the streets of my own neighborhood without armed bodyguards?"

I've remembered this warning many times as, year after year, I have watched the middle class in our country shrink in size, with many falling into the category of the poor or the nearly poor. In 2005, for example, the average income of the top 1 percent of Americans grew to more than $1.1 million, an increase of about 14 percent, while the average income for the bottom 90 percent of Americans actually dropped by 6 percent! A recent editorial in the *New York Times* carried a menacing headline: "It Didn't End Well Last Time." The piece went on to say, "Not since the Roaring Twenties have the rich been so much richer than everyone else." In 2003, the top 1 percent of Americans received 21.8 percent of the nation's income, their largest share since 1929.[1]

The top 10 percent of Americans now collect almost 50 percent of our entire national income, while the remaining 90 percent receive the other half. By contrast, under Democratic and Republican presidents alike— Roosevelt, Truman, Eisenhower, Kennedy, Johnson, and Nixon, from 1942 to 1972—the share of income going to the top 10 percent remained in the 30 to 32 percent range.

Since 1972 the picture has changed dramatically. Over the last three decades the median household income has risen by only $6,400, while the income for the highest 25 percent has increased by $58,000. The super-rich have fared best of all. In 2005 the top one-tenth of 1 percent reported an average income of $5.6 million, up $908,000 in one year, and the top one-hundredth of 1 percent reported annual income averages of $25.7 million—up $4.4 million in one year! Conservatives and liberals, Democrats and Republicans, all should be concerned by this development. Few of us believe that socialism is a workable or desirable system. I certainly do not. Nor do I approve of the politics of class warfare. A national spirit of unity is undermined by politicians who try to pit one economic group against another in order to gain votes for themselves.

As a senator I agreed with President Ronald Reagan that when federal and state tax rates together take more than 90 percent of every extra dollar earned, all incentive is lost for people to work harder to grow the economy. At some point, however, the tax breaks become unjustifiable, and the burden on the middle class gets too heavy to bear. How can anyone justify what has happened to salaries for CEOs in the United States in the past thirty-five years? In 1970 the average CEO made 43 times that of his or her average employee. By 1980 that number rose to 84. By 2005 the average CEO was making 364 times as much as the average employee.[2] Recently, Warren Buffett, one of the wealthiest men in America, who is contributing the bulk of his wealth to a charitable foundation, said, "My class is winning, but they shouldn't be."[3] He obviously understands the importance of preserving a strong middle class and the threat of looming class warfare. Continuing to pursue an economic policy driven by greed will destroy us socially.

The relative tax burden on wage earners is further increased because the Internal Revenue Service is able to collect an estimated 99 percent of taxes based on wage income but captures only about 70 percent of taxes based on business and investment income, which flows mostly to upper-income individuals. While income disparity grows, the basic costs for middle-income families, who spend a large portion of their incomes on health care and education for their children, are also increasing rapidly.

Self-employed middle-income families often face a choice between paying mortgages, educating their children, and paying the premiums for health insurance for themselves. Some time ago the father-in-law of one of our university staff members was forced to have a heart bypass operation. He had no health insurance. He was too young for Medicare. He had worked hard all his life as a carpenter and had never received any kind of public assistance. He paid his taxes and his mortgage payments on time. He helped provide education beyond high school for his five children. At the end of each month, he simply did not have enough money to purchase health insurance for himself. As the hospital bills came in for his heart procedure, they totaled thousands of dollars. He worried that he might lose his home. He didn't want to be a financial burden to his children, because they were starting their own families. After he recovered from his heart surgery, he suffered an appendicitis attack. Though he was in intense pain, he told no one because he didn't want to return to the hospital and add to the medical bills he was slowly trying to pay. Only when he lapsed into unconsciousness did his family realize what was wrong. His appendix had already ruptured. He barely survived after several days in intensive care. His story remains vivid in my memory. Surely in this country, a solid citizen should not have to risk death because he cannot find a way to afford health insurance.

As a university president I see firsthand all the pressures on the middle class. College tuition costs are rising rapidly as states fund a smaller and smaller percentage of the costs of public higher education. I constantly feel a strong moral obligation to raise more scholarship funds to help offset the rising costs, especially for middle-income families. If we fail to keep higher education affordable for middle-income families, we will reduce the lifetime earning opportunities for their children, causing the middle class to shrink even more quickly.

In the years following World War II, middle-class children believed they could accomplish anything if they worked hard enough. Now, as they see the life of the superrich constantly described in the media, and as they watch their parents struggle just to get by, they suffer a loss of self-esteem and hope for their own lives. We are losing that sense of possibility that has made us a great country.

What can we do to restore the strength of the middle class? A more progressive tax structure is part of the answer. Increased tax rates on the highest incomes and increased taxation of luxury items would help. It is shocking that for the first time in our history we have lowered tax burdens on the very wealthy during a war. The resulting increased budget deficits have also created pressure to cut health and educational benefits for poor and middle-income families even further.

In addition to shifting the tax burdens, an expansion of federal scholarships for higher education is needed. Most federal scholarship grants are targeted to help the very poor. Eligibility must be expanded to include middle-income families. It must be scholarships, *not* loans. More student loans alone are not the answer, because too many middle-income students already leave college with debt burdens that limit their future opportunities.

Beyond changing the tax structure and providing more federal college scholarships, it is morally imperative that we provide universal health insurance coverage for all Americans. Market-based approaches such as that now being tried in Massachusetts have great merit. In other states where per capita incomes are lower and more people are without health insurance, larger federal subsidies will be required.

We must not rule out considering a new approach that moves away from the current employer-based system. From 2000 to 2006, the number of people covered by employer plans dropped by more than two million. Competition often forces employers to drop or limit plans, which means that cost-saving preventive medical actions are not encouraged. A competitive plan with subsidies to ensure coverage for low- and middle-income individuals and families, like that recently unveiled by the Council on Economic Development, deserves serious consideration.[4]

Those who have health insurance are already paying the costs for the uninsured, who often end up in hospital emergency rooms. These subsidies are already being paid but in the least-effective way possible. The uninsured wait to get help until they reach a medical crisis. This drives costs higher. There is no excuse for another presidential term to end without implementing universal health insurance. It can be done without using a huge new government bureaucracy as the delivery mechanism. It is time to recognize that our inaction is immoral.

Some politicians have told us that government is the answer to all of our problems. Others have said that government itself is the problem. Neither extreme point of view is correct. Government has a limited role to play, but in some situations responsive and responsible government action is absolutely necessary. It is both appropriate and necessary for government to maintain law and order and to help fund public education. Appropriate government policies can do much to strengthen and enlarge the middle class. By reducing the relative tax burden on middle-income families and helping to reduce the cost of the necessities that they must buy, such as education for their children and health care for their families, we can reverse the shrinkage of the middle class. A strong middle class is essential to America's continued greatness, and preserving it through public and private cooperation must become a national priority.

CHAPTER SIX

The Urgency of Memory

Earlier in this letter I quoted a speech by Bruce Cole, delivered in 2002 when he was chair of the National Endowment for the Humanities. He chose as the title of his lecture "The Urgency of Memory." He was speaking at a conference at New York University that focused on the relevance of the study of the humanities in the aftermath of the 9/11 terrorist attacks.[1]

Cole stated: "The values implicit in the studies of the humanities are part of why we were attacked. The free and fearless exchange of ideas, respect for individual conscience and belief in the power of education. . . . All these things are anathema to our country's enemies. Understanding and affirming these principles is part of the battle."

He continued his thoughtful and powerful remarks by saying, "Today, it is all the more urgent that we study American institutions, culture, and history. Defending our democracy demands more than successful military campaigns. It also requires an understanding of the ideals, ideas, and institutions that have shaped our country. The humanities tell us who we are as a people and why our country is worth fighting for."

I can only affirm Cole's eloquent words. Understanding our history and our values is perhaps more important for Americans than for any national group. Most nations are defined in almost tribal terms. Generally they are made up of people who have lived together in the same geographical place for a long time. They share the same national language and usually the same religion or spiritual outlook. They come from the same cultural tradition.

The United States is a different kind of nation. Many Americans are immigrants or children of immigrants, are of varied races, adhere to different religions, and have richly diverse cultural backgrounds. What makes us Americans is our common set of values and a shared commitment to the political institutions that preserve them.

We cannot defend these ideas or protect the vitality of our institutions, including our constitutional government, unless we understand their origins and how they have evolved over time. We cannot intelligently participate in the current debates about the limits of governmental power and the importance of the independent judicial process unless we understand our history. We cannot protect the liberties guaranteed in our Bill of Rights unless we know what they are and why they were added as amendments to our constitution. James Madison was right when he said, "The diffusion of knowledge is the only true guardian of liberty."

For each of us, it is our life story that gives us our identity. What we have experienced—our personal histories—define us. If you were to lose your personal story, you would lose your personhood. The same is true for our national story. If we forget it, we lose our vision, our identity, our national soul. Our national story unifies us, strengthens us, and inspires us. This generation will have failed America if we let our national story die with us. We must pass it on.

Yet, in this crucial moment in time, Americans seem to know less and less about the history that has created our identity. A recent study of students at fifty-five leading universities found that more than a third were unable to identify the Constitution as the document that establishes the division of powers in our government.[2] A National Assessment of Education Progress test found that more than half of high school seniors could not identify whom or what we fought against in World War II.[3]

Another study found that 60 percent of the American people think that the president, not Congress, has the power to declare war, and 50 percent think that the president can suspend the Constitution whenever he decides to do so. In a study of college students commissioned by the Intercollegiate Studies Institute (ISI), nearly half of the participants did not know that the Federalist Papers were written in support of ratifying the Constitution. Forty-eight percent believed that the Revolutionary War concluded at the Battle of Gettysburg. While only 34 percent knew that George Washington was an American general at the Battle of Yorktown, 98 percent could identify rap singer Snoop Doggy Dogg. Another shocking aspect of the study was the finding that at sixteen of the nation's leading universities, including Brown, Georgetown, Yale, Cornell, Berkeley, and Johns Hopkins, seniors knew less than freshman about American history, foreign affairs, and government.[4]

Why have we become so ignorant of our own history? How has this happened? The ISI study puts the answer very clearly—students do not learn what colleges and schools do not teach. The American Council of Trustees and Alumni followed up by examining the graduation requirements of America's top fifty-five liberal arts colleges and research universities as ranked by *U.S. News & World Report*. Shockingly, none of these elite institutions specifically required that students take a course in American history to graduate. In addition, 78 percent of the institutions surveyed did not require students to take any history at all. The report concluded, "The best that can be said is that students are permitted to take history to satisfy other requirements in areas such as social sciences or diversity."

We cannot preserve and protect the Constitution unless we know what it says and why it was drafted in the way it was. I suspect that even many members of Congress, and perhaps even a few of our presidents, have lacked the understanding necessary to fulfill the oaths they take to preserve the Constitution.

When the Soviets were the first to launch a space satellite, known as Sputnik, during the 1950s, the reaction in this country was immediate and widespread. There was concern that we might be falling behind the Russians in math and science. As a result, national and local initiatives were begun to improve the teaching of science and mathematics from elementary schools to university graduate schools.

These recent reports, which reflect that we as a people don't fully understand who we are and where we came from, should evoke at least an equal determination to act. We must do more than build beautiful memorials to Thomas Jefferson in the nation's capital. We must heed his words: "If a nation expects to be ignorant and free . . . it expects what never was and never will be."

Not surprisingly, the studies I have mentioned found that the knowledge of our history was highest at those colleges where the largest percentage of students were taking courses in American history and government. It is time for a national crusade to confront this crisis in citizenship! We should begin by examining the curriculum at K–12 schools and improve it. College and university graduation requirements must be changed to include the study of American history and government at the college level in order to graduate.

In addition, we need to establish more centers of national stature to improve the teaching of American history at the K–12 level and more centers of scholarship and research at colleges and universities to expand the knowledge of our past and to enliven the debate about the ideas that formed our system of government. The Colonial Williamsburg Foundation provides excellent residential and online courses for secondary teachers in colonial history. The teachers who participate are reinvigorated by the stimulating discussions and courses. That excitement is passed on to their students, and it awakens in them a new interest in their own history. We need more such programs to involve many more teachers. Colleges and universities should provide summer institutes to enrich the backgrounds of those teaching in elementary and secondary schools. The National Endowment for the Humanities also funds such beneficial efforts through the Landmarks of American History and Culture Workshops for Schoolteachers and We the People programs.

The same energy and vitality must return to college campuses. Only a tiny handful of research and study programs at American universities focus on the ideas and events that helped to produce the U.S. Constitution. One of these is the James Madison Program at Princeton. Many more such centers are needed if we are to make American history and culture a widespread topic of discussion and curiosity in the broader society. Recently, historians such as David McCullough have written masterful books that have caused larger numbers of Americans to focus on the people and conditions that led to our existence as an independent nation.

If we are to debate current political issues intelligently, and indeed to vote intelligently, we must share the common frame of reference that has sustained our free society for so many generations. The understanding of our history needs to be as broad as possible. American literature and the creative arts must be included. They have held up a mirror to our society, enabling us to better understand what Americans have experienced in the past.

The eighteenth-century Scottish poet Robert Burns wrote that it is a great gift to see ourselves as others see us. Those who have come from other places have given us new insights into ourselves. Alexis de Tocqueville, the Frenchman who traveled across America and wrote about American democracy in 1835, has given us an analysis of the factors that contributed to our national greatness. His words are as relevant today as they were two hundred years ago.

Tocqueville noted that America had a tradition of volunteerism found in few other societies. Perhaps co-operative action by neighbors was born out of the frontier experience. He noted that when one American sees a problem, he walks across the road to discuss it with his neighbor, and the two go together to other neighbors. In a short time they have formed an organization or a committee to address the problem—all without government being involved. That spirit is still very much alive in this country. We lead the world in hours of volunteer service and charitable contributions to our communities.

In his book *Bowling Alone*, Harvard sociologist Robert Putnam focuses on the important role played by volunteers and private organizations in our society. He chose his title to serve as a symbolic expression of what happens when we do not unite together for a common purpose. He tells the story of two men who were from different walks of life and were not likely to have known each other. They joined the same bowling league and became friends. One had a serious illness. He faced death. The other ended up donating one of his kidneys to save the life of his friend. Had they not come together, and had the man who became ill gone bowling alone, it is likely that he would not have lived. Working together, coming together, and creating real communities all give life to a society. Putnam found, however, that in recent decades the number of volunteer organizations has sharply declined. In the 1980s and 1990s, attendance at the meetings of organizations he studied declined by 50 percent. He even found that Americans spent less time visiting with each other in their homes. In twenty years the number of Americans who said they visited the homes of friends at least once each week fell from 66 percent to 33 percent.

There are many reasons for that decline. We are a much more mobile society, in grave danger of becoming rootless. Because we move often, we sometimes avoid investing the time to truly get to know our neighbors, let alone get involved in community activities.

Our work habits, long hours spent away from our homes, and long commutes to the workplace leave us exhausted when we reach home at the end of the day. We are simply ready to close the garage door when we enter our homes and never even get to know our neighbors. The workplace becomes our neighborhood, and our coworkers become our only community and extended family. That is why there is so much angst in America about the possible loss of jobs due to corporate restructuring. A person who loses his job in some ways loses his neighborhood, his extended family, and even his identity.

With our increasing mobility we also no longer live close to our extended families. Loss of intergenerational relationships and friendships is part of the cost of economic efficiency. We are often around people only of our same economic and social status and find it more difficult to "walk a mile in someone else's shoes." The decline of public schools attended by a broad cross section of young people from different stations in life has further narrowed the range of our shared experiences.

Shared experience is the basis for strong communities. At times in my classes I share with my students references to my own childhood. I grew up in a stable small town where the same families had lived together for many years. While I didn't always appreciate it when I was younger, adults in our small community looked after other people's children as well as their own. Even minor transgressions on my part reached the ears of my parents before I could confess them myself. So many lessons in life were taught to me in discussions I had with friends who were the age of my parents but with whom I felt far more comfortable in discussing personal subjects than I would have felt with my own parents. Every Sunday after church we drove nine miles to have lunch with my maternal grandparents and my great-grandmother. Aunts and uncles and cousins were gathered around the table, and we shared stories of family and community history. Later in the afternoon, we drove fifteen miles in the other direction to have dinner with my other set of grandparents, and repeated the same rituals with them and with my father's extended family.

As I spoke in class about what it was like to grow up in a real community surrounded by family and learning and growing from intergenerational friendships, I was struck by the intense and often emotional reaction of my students. At times I saw tears well up in their eyes. Using different words, the common theme of their response was: "I wish I could have had a childhood like yours."

We have to consciously work harder to rebuild the spirit of community. One of my goals as a university president is to use the college years when students live closely together to create such a true community. For some students, college represents their first opportunity to experience what it is like to live in a real community where we assume responsibility for each other.

Every decision should be made with the goal of increasing community. Outdoor spaces and gardens with benches need to be designed to function as inviting outdoor "rooms" to bring people together for conversation. Residential dormitories need to become homes with faculty families living physically with students in a way that invites intergenerational friendships and discussions. We must assure that rooming decisions are made in ways that bring students from diverse backgrounds together so they can grow by being around people unlike themselves.

While ethnic and cultural groups will naturally form separate organizations, there is a strong need to bring them together to work on common projects and to be physically housed close to each other. Buildings need to be designed to encourage shared interdisciplinary spaces. There must be a "heart of the campus"—usually the student union—that fills the functions of the small-town drugstore or favorite local cafe, where everyone passes through each day to visit with each other and to find out what is going on in the community. At the University of Oklahoma we have a "Cousins" program through which United States students adopt international students as their "cousins" and volunteer to spend social time together. After experiencing these real communities on university campuses, many of our students will then go on to build strong communities where they live after they graduate.

Racial and other stereotypes break down as students get to know each other as individuals. It inspires me to see how much our students care about each other and take care of each other. These connections also lead to greater civility in our community—a quality so much needed in our national discourse. At the entrance to our campus are words I once heard spoken by Guido Calebresi, dean emeritus of Yale Law School: "A university is a place where we should learn how to argue and debate with each other without ceasing to love and respect each other." Our nation will reflect those values only if we actively teach them by word and practice in our schools.

Of all my experiences as a university president, I will never forget the day when a student stood up in my large lecture class and shared his life experiences with his fellow students. We were discussing the welfare cycle and how to help future generations escape it. The student asked me if he could address the class. He was a partially deaf football player who wore hearing aids in his helmet. Volunteers came to class with him to make sure he did not miss major points in his note-taking. He began by saying that the subject under discussion was not an abstract one for him but was a real part of his life. He described how as a child he suffered physical abuse and was taken by a child welfare agency from his home to live in orphanages and foster homes. "I never had a family until I came to the University of Oklahoma," he said. He spoke about his coaches and teachers who invited him to their homes and spent time mentoring him. He continued, "I have never observed a holiday alone. My fellow students have always been there for me like brothers and sisters to celebrate my successes with me and to help pick me up when I was down." He concluded, "Thank you for being my family." I could not continue with the class even though time remained on the clock. This student had put into words what I hoped we could accomplish at our university. His honest eloquence moved many of us to tears.

Working to revitalize our spirit of community and the spirit of volunteerism must go hand in hand with a new focus on understanding our history and institutions. Even though we realize that our nation cannot survive if we do not prepare succeeding generations to be knowledgeable and involved citizens, it will not be easy to convince schools to take limited resources and use them to increase the teaching of American history and culture.

The goal of higher education today is largely to teach skills that will produce direct economic benefit. I have already written about the importance of teaching math, science, and technology. We must retain our competitive edge economically. However, presidents, chancellors, and boards of regents must have the courage to insist that the teaching of other courses must not come at the expense of teaching about our own history and culture. If we learn nothing of our own history, literature, and creative arts, we will become what one friend of mine called "a nation of skilled barbarians."

I have also in this letter called attention to the need for American education to do more to encourage the study of other cultures and promote study abroad. It is imperative that we increase our understanding of the rest of the world. However, we must not trade off the study of American history and government in order to do so.

Political correctness and a desire to satisfy every academic discipline by assigning equal importance to all courses of study have led colleges and universities to do away with a specific list of core courses to be taken to receive degrees. The recent "Spellings Report," issued by the U.S. Secretary of Education's Commission on the Future of Higher Education, sidestepped the need for a defined core curriculum in American colleges and universities. This compromise frees each faculty member to do his or her "own thing" without anyone taking responsibility for the creation of a shared body of knowledge that all of us come to know so that we can function as a coherent society.

We have sidestepped the obvious need for core requirements essential to civic literacy, because we do not want to set off controversies between races, genders, and ethnic groups about what we should require all students to study. We can no longer allow these "culture wars" to paralyze us. We must take action.

Above all, whatever our vocations or areas of specialty, all of us are citizens. Harvard professor Harry R. Lewis wrote recently that "institutions for higher education have a social contract with America. We owe it to the country to teach our students how democracy works."[5]

It is time for universities to meet their responsibility

to the society that has given them the freedom and resources to exist. Every college in America should require students to have college credits in American history and American government on their transcripts as a condition for receiving degrees.

A nation that does not know how it became great will not remain great.

CHAPTER SEVEN

The Question

Thank you for allowing me to share with you the thoughts contained in this letter. If this letter simply helps begin a civil and thoughtful national discussion about things that should really matter to us, it will have served its purpose.

In closing, let us return to the question that was asked of the Rhodes Scholarship candidates: How long will the United States remain the world's leading superpower?

None of us knows for sure. Unlike historical determinists who believe that powers beyond our control will determine our destiny, I believe the outcome is largely in our own hands. While we face serious challenges, we begin with a large head start in almost every area. Even with terrorist threats, we are among the safest nations in the world. Unlike those who live in battle zones, we rarely think about being killed or losing our loved ones in the course of a day's activity. Intellectually we are still the world's leaders in higher education, research, and technology. While we must work to rebuild the commitment to community, we lead the world by a large margin in voluntary activity. Our economic standard of living, measured in real terms, is still the best in the world for the average American. Our political system, even with all its current defects, is not in danger of dissolving into anarchy or revolution. We are still the nation that more immigrants wish to enter than any other, and we need to remind ourselves that the talents and values of every new group of immigrants over the past four hundred years have made us stronger and better.

The history of our nation is one of almost unbroken progress. While there have been temporary ups and downs, each generation has been able to say it has left America better in most ways than it found it.

The World War II generation has been lauded by many as "the greatest generation." It certainly deserves the designation as one of the greatest. When it comes to honoring greatness, however, we must never forget the generation of our Founders. Historian Gordon Wood argues that a unique combination of factors produced a first generation of leaders of such remarkable wisdom, foresight, and civility that they will never be surpassed.

We must face the real possibility that we could be the first generation of Americans that fails to contribute to the unbroken line of progress in our country. I hope that even such a suggestion will shake us out of our apathy. To me it is un-American to resign ourselves to a life for our children that is not as good or better than our own.

We must not sulk in the corner when confronted with unpleasant facts such as the world's declining respect for us. Instead, we must constantly have the courage to ask, "Why?" When we make progress in finding the answers, we must care enough about the outcome to spring into action. At the risk of sounding jingoistic, I truly believe that the world will be a better place in the twenty-first century if America continues to play a leadership role.

In some ways the challenge we face is more complex than that faced by the World War II generation. While the bipartisan blueprint put together by the leaders of that generation to guide us through the Cold War seems somewhat self-evident in hindsight, it was certainly not easy to devise at the time. Implementing the Marshall Plan alone was an exceptional accomplishment that took incredible vision and generosity of spirit.

Still, Hitler's fascism and Soviet Communism were more easily identified and understood adversaries than those we face today. A common understanding of the threats made it easier in the past to organize a united response. Today we are faced with a threat that does not admit to a single definition. The black-and-white world of the Cold War has given way to a world with many shades of gray. It includes long-standing religious and ethnic divisions; very different levels of economic progress in various parts of the world; grudges based on a perceived lack of respect; and environmental, health, and law-enforcement challenges that know no national boundaries. It is a world in which weapons of mass destruction and the capacity to inflict catastrophic damage have fallen into the hands of groups much less likely to make rational decisions than the nation-states that decided about the use of their power during the Cold War.

This newly complex set of challenges comes at a time when the United States as a single nation will continue to have an ever-declining share of the world's military and economic strength. This does not mean we will not continue to have perhaps the greatest military and economic strength, but rather that we will not have a predominant share of strength. Our moral strength and the influence of our ideals of freedom and human dignity need not be diminished if we are careful to protect them and live up to them.

At times we have confused "leadership" with "dominance." Our current president, for example, has opted for using our unilateral military strength as a preferred method of dealing with crises. Instead, military action, especially action by ourselves, should be used only when economic and diplomatic action in cooperation with others have been tried first.

Before we can be in a position to determine our proper role in the world, we must first better understand ourselves and strengthen ourselves at home. As stated earlier, we cannot remain great if we do not understand what made us great. We must not be stampeded in times of crisis into compromising the rights and civil liberties for which so many Americans have given their lives.

When we start to ponder how to maintain our influence with the rest of the world, we sometimes park our common sense at the door. We all understand the power of example. As children we learn less from what is said about how we should conduct ourselves than from how we see our parents and others behave. The example of the fairness and vitality of our own society will do more than anything else to maintain our influence in a world where others will have military and economic strengths of their own.

We must improve our ability to listen. While the world may not yet be truly multipolar and while we may for a limited time have predominant strength, we should use this time to create new institutions that will serve us well when the situation changes, when we have one of the seats at the decision-making table but no longer hold most of the cards.

In other words, we should treat emerging powers with the respect we would show to any equal partner. We should act now as if a multipolar world had already evolved and not wait to change our policies until that change has actually taken place. For example, we should work hard to develop joint projects with the Chinese in areas where we have agreement. No single relationship will be more important to the peace and stability of the world in this century than the relationships between the United States and China. If we allow ourselves to become adversaries, we could face a situation far more dangerous than we faced in the Cold War with the Soviet Union.

The new form of leadership that we must embrace will in some ways provide our nation with an even more challenging, creative, and rewarding role. Real leaders do not operate primarily through command and control. No leaders truly accomplish anything worthwhile by themselves. We achieve more when we share credit and ownership with others. We need to pull together the best ideas from all sources and implement them. Even in a multipolar world, however, there must be a consistent leader and catalyst for group action. That leader should be the United States. Our leadership must be based upon affection and mutual respect and not upon the necessity of yielding to power.

We must be prepared to talk with and listen to all other nations, including those that appear to be hostile. Conditions change and alliances constantly shift. Politicians often speak of the wisdom of keeping our tent as large as possible. Talking with adversaries is always valuable because it helps us better understand their intentions and better prepare for their actions. Even when we have major disagreements with others, we should seek to find points of agreement and initiate joint projects that naturally build bonds, making it easier to avoid conflict.

We live in a world that is far more complex, interrelated, and fast-changing than the world of our parents and grandparents. Because of the nature of the times in which we live, we must be sure that we build our strength in the basic areas that matter while we still have the chance to do so.

Nassim Nicholas Taleb has written a recent best-selling book titled *The Black Swan: The Impact of the Highly Improbable.* As nearly all swans are white, it is a sudden surprise when we encounter a black one. Taleb uses the black swan as a symbol of the unpredictable, sudden event that has a major impact on us. We experience these events in our personal lives. An unexpected meeting with the person who becomes the object of our deepest love and becomes our mate for life is an example. The stock market crash of 1929 and the 9/11 terrorist attacks are examples of unexpected events that have an enormous effect upon the entire world.

Taleb argues that as we have moved from a stable agrarian society to a fast-paced technological global society with populations concentrated in urban areas, the impact of these unexpected events grows larger. These events also seem to occur more often because events that might create only a small ripple in a simpler time can create widespread havoc in our interdependent world with instant communications.

In a way, Taleb is saying the same thing that former British prime minister Margaret Thatcher once said to me. I asked her to describe the most important lesson she had learned through her many years as a political leader. She responded with no hesitation, "Always expect the unexpected."

Living in a quickly changing and unpredictable world means that we must be prepared for the unexpected. How can we do that? The answer is in some ways as simple as the Scout motto, "Be prepared." To be prepared we need to be strong at home. We need to make sure we know who we are and what we believe. We must be highly trained and educated. We must not be so leveraged economically that we lack the resources to respond to the unexpected crisis. Having many friends also helps when confronting an emergency, and for us as a nation, that means strong, reliable friends all around the world. As life becomes more unpredictable, taking care of the basics becomes ever more important.

We will have to be even more creative than most earlier generations of Americans if we intend to continue our leadership. That challenge is exciting and invigorating. We can meet it!

Even with all of our problems and shortcomings, the United States is still legitimately viewed as the land of opportunity. Around the world, people are standing in line to enter this country. It has an energy and vitality that is unequaled. The creative spirit of America is reflected in many ways—from developing an unparalleled number of new patents and new technologies to the imaginative improvisation of American art forms like jazz.

While we must work to preserve it, no nation allows greater upward social mobility than ours. Social standing and economic opportunity are not limited by family history. Character and work ethic count for more. We also have made diversity a source of strength in our society. Most nations have found it difficult to absorb waves of immigration into their countries. In the United States we have become stronger with every new group that has come to America. From the Irish who fled the potato famine, to the Jews who escaped the Holocaust, to the Vietnamese who came in the 1970s after the war, to those coming today, our new Americans have contributed their talents and hard work to make our country even greater.

I have a good friend who lives in Tulsa, Oklahoma. His name is Ri Le. He fled Vietnam as the communists took over by ditching his helicopter at sea near an American ship that picked him up. He eventually made his way to Oklahoma, where he worked more than twenty hours each day for several months as an aircraft mechanic to save enough money to open a very successful restaurant. He has helped bring other members of his family to America. All four of his children have gone to college. Even after thirty years in the restaurant business he still rises every morning at six and rarely gets home until midnight. He is known for giving back to charities in his community. To me, Ri Le is not only a friend but a great American. Any nation in the world would be lucky to have him as a member of its national family. He chose America.

We still lead the world in volunteerism and charitable giving. In our dynamic society, we do not want the government to solve our problems for us. It is that goodness described by Tocqueville—a reaching-out to help others—that is a source of our national greatness. That sprit is alive and well. In 2006, 61 million Americans gave more than 8 billion hours to volunteer activities, up 6 percent since 1989.[1] Children, youth, and college students are volunteering at twice the national rate. They reinforce my faith in this country.

In all of the ways that matter, we Americans have so many reasons to believe that our future can be even greater than our past. Would you change places with the members of any generation at any other time in history? Would you change places with those who live in any other nation? I would not. I hope you feel the same way. Together, let us embrace the future with all its possibilities!

Sincerely,

Daniel Boren

Postscript

November 1, 2010

Three years have passed since I wrote the letter you have just finished reading. At that time I wrote, "The country we love is in trouble. In truth we are in grave danger of declining as a nation. If we do not act quickly, that decline will become dramatic." I indicated that if I had been mailing the letter to you in an envelope, I would have marked it URGENT. Today, our situation is even more critical.

Much has happened in the past three years. A new president and a new Congress have been elected, but they have not succeeded in changing the fundamental direction of our country.

Never before in American history have we cut taxes during a war. In the past, Americans have willingly paid war taxes and made other sacrifices for our national security. The cost of the two major wars in Iraq and Afghanistan is approaching $2 trillion, yet we have made no provision to pay for them.

The prolonged lack of oversight of the growing risks in the financial markets caught up with us, and the stock market collapsed, losing almost half of its value in three months.

The failure to regulate the financial sector coupled

with the failure to pay for the two wars undermined the economy and led to the most severe recession since the Great Depression. Joblessness reached 10 percent.

America's share of the world's economy continued to decline by about 1 percent each year.

The middle class continued to shrink. Meanwhile the top 1 percent of the population in income received more than 29 percent of the nation's income last year, the highest percentage since 1928.

Respect for the United States around the world rebounded somewhat after the presidential elections, but regained only half of the ground lost during the administration of President George W. Bush.

When faced with major challenges, Americans have always found a way to come together. We have rallied behind nonpartisan solutions and strategies. This time, we have failed to do so. Partisan polarization and political bickering are sapping our strength. We seem to have forgotten Abraham Lincoln's warning that a house divided against itself cannot stand.

The two greatest threats to America's future, are partisanship and pessimism.

Partisanship continues to stop action on crucial parts of the national agenda. When our government does finally act, as it did on health care, for example, the outcome is far from ideal. Many in one party have refused to work with the other party to develop consensus solutions. They have largely just said "no." This makes it even more difficult to obtain the sixty-vote supermajority required in the U.S. Senate to end filibusters and pass major bills. To get to sixty votes, managers of bills are forced to strike outrageously unwise deals with holdout senators. The deals result in flawed programs and policies. In times of economic stress, our country cannot afford anything less than the wisest and most cost-effective outcomes. That is not what we are getting. At the same time, areas of critical importance to our future such as education get largely ignored because so much time and attention are wasted on useless bickering between the two political parties. Both parties share the blame.

With now less than 6 percent of the world's population, the United States must have the best-educated and most highly skilled workforce in the world if we are to remain a major influence. Yet we have slipped further behind in the past three years. A decade ago, the United States was the world's leader in producing young people with college bachelor's degrees—a key indicator of long-term economic strength. Today, according to the College Board, the United States has slipped to twelfth place, with only 40 percent of twenty-two- to thirty-year-olds earning college degrees. Canada leads the world with almost 56 percent, and South Korea is close behind. According to the Organization for Economic Cooperation and Development, the United States also remains far behind in K–12 education, ranking twenty-fifth in math and twenty-first in science.

Our leaders missed a great opportunity during the recent economic crisis to create jobs through a massive program to rebuild America's aging infrastructure. This critical area has received too little attention and inadequate investment over the past three decades. The rupture of a major gas pipeline in San Bruno, California, which caused the destruction of an entire neighborhood, is just one indicator that neglecting our infrastructure carries a high cost. The American people would have overwhelmingly supported an even larger stimulus package if we had been certain that the spending was going for something we really need.

Partisan divisions also kept us from taking action to halt explosive increases in annual budget deficits and the national debt. Our national debt has already reached the highest level in our history and is expected to reach a level equal to our entire GDP by 2011, according to the Congressional Budget Office. Paying the interest on this debt, let alone reducing it, will be a crushing burden on our children and grandchildren. Warren Buffet has warned that unless we act to curtail deficit spending, the United States will lose its reputation for financial integrity. If that happens, we will face incalculable risks. Those who live in other countries could decide to stop investing their savings in our country. If they stop holding our debt, it could undermine the value of our currency and send our interest rates sky-high. The impact would bring about the collapse of our economy.

Over three-fourths of the deficit results from the refusal of the political leadership to ask Americans to help pay for the two recent wars and from continued runaway spending on entitlements such as Social Security, government pensions, Medicare, and Medicaid. Neither political party is willing to take responsible action to raise taxes or cut entitlements spending for fear that the other party will blame them. The American people are smart enough to know that we cannot live beyond our means forever. In fact, we are waiting for political leaders to come forward who will ask us to make a shared sacrifice on a fair basis. Most of us are willing to make sacrifices as long as we know that all of us are helping as much as we can. Instead of appealing to our patriotism and challenging us to think about what we can do for our country, too many current politicians blatantly appeal to our self-interest. They promise us all we want but without asking us to pay for it.

We have also missed the opportunity to make a prudent drawdown of our military forces in Afghanistan. The American people are ahead of our leaders. We know that no country has ever been able to occupy Afghanistan. Alexander the Great tried it. The British and the Russians tried it. They all failed. Afghan history demonstrates that the people of that country want tribal autonomy and not a strong central government. Geography and a 90 percent illiteracy rate make the creation of an American-style democratic government impossible to achieve in our lifetime. In an apt analogy, the writer Fareed Zakaria once wisely reminded us that it doesn't make sense to try to plant palm trees in Canada. It takes the right set of conditions to make it possible for political structures like ours to succeed.

Our original mission in Afghanistan was to shut down training areas for the terrorist group Al Qaeda. Our mission was not to occupy the country or to build a new kind of Afghan nation. Published reports estimate that there are now only about a hundred members of Al Qaeda in Afghanistan. If the stamping out of Al Qaeda is our goal, it makes no sense to send 150,000 American troops to do it. A small, versatile strike force could keep these terrorists in check. With a cost of $1 million per year for each soldier deployed, the United States by itself cannot afford to be the world's policeman. We are financially and militarily overstretched. The financial resources now being spent in Afghanistan are desperately needed at home in the United States to rebuild our national strength. The money being spent in military involvement overseas could more than pay for important improvements in education and infrastructure. Above all, the tragic loss of brave young Americans in an effort that can never succeed is inexcusable.

The American people understand that poisonous partisanship has kept us from responding decisively to our challenges. Self-described independents are the fastest-growing group in the United States. Some studies even show that independent-leaning voters are a larger group than either Democrats or Republicans. The Tea Party movement is but one manifestation of a larger sense of political alienation across the entire political spectrum. It is not hard to understand why many Americans are fed up with both the Democratic and Republican parties. There is something far more important than either party. It is called the United States of America.

Excessive partisanship helps to fuel the second major threat—pessimism. Americans have a feeling of helplessness just when we need a national can-do spirit. If we give up, the national pessimism about our future will become a self-fulfilling prophecy. Never in our history have Americans given up! Let us resolve that we never will!

I began my letter to you by sharing an experience I had in interviewing Rhodes scholarship candidates. Almost ten years ago, I asked this extremely bright group of college seniors how long they thought the United States would remain the world's greatest superpower. They sat in stunned silence. They wanted to blurt out "Forever!" as their answer. Our declining national performance and our changed status in the world had not yet become conscious concerns for them. Their failure to focus on the magnitude of the challenge facing us deeply troubled me.

Late in 2010, I repeated the same question to my freshman honors class at the University of Oklahoma. Many of the students in the seminar were National Merit Scholars. Their answers ranged from those who believed we would lose our status as the world's leading nation within ten years to one or two who thought our decline would take more than fifty years. No one believed we would be dominant in world affairs by the end of this century. The class consensus predicted about thirty more years of U.S. leadership.

I was stunned to see such an enormous change in perception from our best and brightest young people in less than a decade. In one sense, it was reassuring to see their level of understanding of our national situation and to see them focused on our problems rather than oblivious to them. Yet their answers in some ways concern me even more than those of their peers did ten years ago. They reflect the pessimism of national polls showing that the great majority of Americans feel that our future will not be as great as our past.

At a deeper level, their responses also reflect a view that there is not much we can do to reverse our decline as long as our political leaders continue to fight with each other instead of solving our problems. In their view, the political process is broken.

Political polarization is currently the greatest cause of our pessimism. If political partisanship is crippling us, it is pessimism that has immobilized us. This is no time to sit cynically on the sidelines. This is a time for action! Our political process is broken, and we must fix it to restore its strengths.

We do not have to accept the status quo. We can change it. Let us begin by analyzing the causes of partisan polarization. Part of it comes from what Bill Bishop calls the "Big Sort" in his book *The Big Sort: Why the Clustering of Like-Minded America Is Tearing Us Apart.* Americans are increasingly choosing to live in neighborhoods and areas with people who think as they do. We attend religious services and club meetings with people like ourselves. We increasingly obtain our news and information from media outlets that reinforce our own biases. When we separate ourselves from one another in these ways, we begin to forget how to live together in the broader society and how to learn from each other. In some ways the polarization of Washington reflects the polarization of our society. This problem has no easy solution. It clearly makes community-wide schooling even more important as a way to ensure that young people from a true cross-section of our society come together. We need to have more community-wide forums and gatherings where we can discuss important issues in a thoughtful and civil manner. One point of intervention remains university campuses, where a strong sense of community can be created amid diversity. I believe that the habits of tolerance and mutual respect formed during the university experience will continue later in life.

While some Americans seem polarized on the right or the left of the political spectrum, most people are still political moderates who want to work together. Why are these bipartisan moderates so underrepresented in Congress?

Part of the problem lies with the way congressional districts are drawn. Majorities in state legislatures generally try to maximize the number of "safe" congressional districts for their own party. According to Bishop's *The Big Sort*, the number of districts that reliably provide a large majority of votes for the candidate of one party or the other has doubled in recent years. To be elected from a "safe" district, the member of Congress needs to appeal only to the most activist members of his or her own party, and not to moderates in the other party or to independents. Those elected in such districts do not go to Congress seeking to be bipartisan. In fact, appearing to be too bipartisan often makes candidates vulnerable to defeat in their own party primaries—a very disturbing recent trend.

Reform of the congressional redistricting process is urgently needed so that more districts are competitive. This in turn will encourage candidates to reach across party lines and seek support from the center. State legislatures could create nonpartisan redistricting commissions. If they do not, a federal constitutional amendment may be in order.

Another cause of excessive partisanship is the way we finance campaigns. Earlier in this letter, I described the corrupting influence on our politics of huge amounts of special interest money. In the past three years, the problem has only grown worse. A tragically misguided decision by the U.S. Supreme Court in 2010 (*Citizens United v. Federal Election Commission*) further opened the floodgates of money flowing from corporations and labor unions. Because some corporate stockholders are not even American citizens, we now have a legal framework that allows them to influence American elections. Cooperation in Congress in the broad national interest is not encouraged when more and more money comes from those with narrow special-interest agendas.

Three years ago I advocated a constitutional amendment on campaign spending. It is needed now more than ever. I advocate capping total campaign spending. In addition, we should adopt a rule that only those eligible to vote in a particular election be allowed to make contributions to candidates. In other words, only citizens of the state and district involved in the election could contribute. No corporations, unions, political action committees (PACs), or out-of-state individuals or groups could do so. How can we maintain grassroots democracy when most of the campaign money is coming from out-of-state interest groups? Should we really be surprised when members of Congress listen to the groups giving them the campaign funds they need to win elections, instead of to the people back home? That is exactly what is happening!

Abolishing the Electoral College could also help diminish extreme partisanship. The Electoral College was created at a time when an accurate national count of votes for president was not possible. Today, we can and do total the national popular vote. In recent elections, Democratic presidential nominees spent no time in "red" states, and Republican nominees did not go to "blue" states, because they had little chance of winning any electoral votes in those states under our winner-take-all system. If candidates were elected by the national popular vote, they would visit more states and involve themselves with all of our citizens in the national political dialogue instead of speaking in person only to those who live in swing states.

In addition, moderates in Congress need to become more proactive. The congressional caucuses for each of the two parties meet regularly to plot strategy for continuing partisan warfare. We need moderates of both parties to meet regularly to work on ways to cooperate to solve our problems.

Presidents need to quit meeting primarily with official party leaders and should avoid delegating the details of crafting crucial legislation to them. Party leaders are often the virtual prisoners of the more extreme groups in their own caucuses. Instead, the president should empower moderates by inviting relatively small, bipartisan congressional working groups to meet directly with him to coauthor consensus proposals.

On another front, it is time to end the filibuster in the U.S. Senate. Until the past three or four decades, the filibuster was rarely used as a partisan weapon. Senators restrained themselves and used the filibuster to prolong debate only on constitutional or other extremely important issues. The filibuster is now used routinely on virtually all controversial issues. To require a sixty-vote supermajority on major bills often requires deal-making with those whose votes are required to get to sixty. Totally unmerited compromises are made. They distort national policy and further disillusion the public with the political process. In these highly polarized times, we can no longer afford to allow filibusters in the U.S. Senate. This is not a partisan issue. Democrats or Republicans, when given a popular mandate to govern, should be able to do so. Filibusters also tend to fuel more partisanship, which is the last thing we need.

Finally, if the vicious cycle of partisanship continues unabated, there could well be an opening for a serious independent candidacy for the presidency in coming elections. Perhaps an independent president would be better able to build a unified consensus. Temporarily changing the political environment might then allow a return to a two-party system capable of functioning as it did in the first eight decades of the twentieth century. If the current situation does not change, it would be worth experimenting with an independent presidency.

None of the reforms will be easy. None will happen overnight. Some would argue that it is unrealistic to even propose them. One thing is certain: these reforms will never happen unless we start talking together about the need for them.

Although our challenges have only grown over the past three years, I remain optimistic. With all of our problems, there is still no other nation with which we would want to change places. Other countries have serious problems, too. Some have populations growing either too rapidly or two slowly. In some countries, democratic institutions are very fragile, and the transition from dictatorship to democracy and free enterprise is extremely difficult. Many countries have severe regional economic imbalances and deep ethnic, religious, or racial divisions. They have legitimate concerns about national security and the threat of military attack. They marvel at Americans' ability to build and maintain a stable, mutually tolerant community amid our great diversity. Above all, we have a society where freedom is maximized. Freedom's transforming power still shapes our future. We must never lose our faith that in the long run, free societies are the ones that will succeed.

My optimism continues to be rooted in the values and spirit of the generations of young Americans represented by my students. They care about each other and about our country. They are already giving back to their communities at historically high levels as volunteers and involved citizens. They are generous, decent, and creative. They have not given up on America, and neither should we. Not now! Not ever!

D.L.B.

Notes

Introduction
1. "Global Unease with Major World Powers," Pew Global Attitudes Project, June 6, 2007.
2. NBC/*Wall Street Journal* poll, July 27, 2006.
3. Bruce Cole, speech at New York University, July 7, 2002.

Chapter 1
1. Pew Global Attitudes Project, June 27, 2007.
2. Churchill quoted in Christopher Catherwood, *Churchill's Folly: How Winston Churchill Created Modern Iraq* (New York: Carroll & Graf, 2004), 202.
3. "The Wind of Change," speech to the South African Parliament, February 3, 1960.
4. *Washington Post,* July 11, 2006.

Chapter 2
1. Princeton Survey Research Associates International, May 22, 2006, study, p. 4.
2. Donald R. Matthews, *U.S. Senators and Their World* (Westport, Conn.: Greenwood Press, 1980).

Chapter 3
1. Arthur M. Schlesinger, Jr., *The Age of Roosevelt* (Boston: Houghton Mifflin, 1957).
2. Center for Responsive Politics, July 7, 2007, report. Dollar figures are actual, not adjusted for inflation.
3. "Leadership PACs," *The Hill,* September 27, 2006.
4. Dean Calbreath, "Commissions Taken on Campaign Cash," *San Diego Union-Tribune,* March 19, 2006.

5. Wertheimer quoted in *Wall Street Journal,* January 12, 1994, p. A12.

Chapter 4

1. Office of Management and Budget, August 13, 2007.
2. Congressional Budget Office, January 31, 2007.
3. *Digest of Education Statistics,* 2006.
4. Concord Coalition Report, *New York Times,* January 5, 2007.
5. Jorn-Statten Pischke, Working Paper 9964, National Bureau of Economic Research, 2003.
6. American Society of Civil Engineers, *2005 Report Card for America's Infrastructure.*

Chapter 5

1. *New York Times,* April 4, 2007.
2. Lou Dobbs, *War on the Middle Class: How the Government, Big Business, and Special Interest Groups Are Waging War on the American Dream and How to Fight Back* (New York: Viking, 2006).
3. CNN.com, June 19, 2005.
4. Research and Policy Committee, Council on Economic Development, "Quality, Affordable Health Care for All," 2007.

Chapter 6

1. Cole, July 7, 2002, speech.
2. *Intelligence Studies Institute Report,* 2000.
3. *San Diego Union,* November 3, 2002.
4. American Council of Trustees and Alumni, February 21, 2000.
5. Harry R. Lewis, "Point of View: A Core Curriculum for Tomorrow's Citizens," *Chronicle Review,* September 7, 2007.

Chapter 7

1. *Time*, August 30, 2007.